GEOSPHERE

The Land and Its Uses

OUR FRAGILE PLANET

Atmosphere

Biosphere

Climate

Geosphere

Humans and the Natural Environment

Hydrosphere

Oceans

Polar Regions

OUR FRAG

GEOSPHERE

The Land and Its Uses

DANA DESONIE, PH.D.

CHELSEA HOUSE
PUBLISHERS
An imprint of Infobase Publishing

Geosphere

Copyright © 2008 by Dana Desonie, Ph.D.

Chelsea House
An imprint of Infobase Publishing
132 West 31st Street
New York NY 10001

Library of Congress Cataloging-in-Publication Data
Desonie, Dana.
  Geosphere : the land and its uses / Dana Desonie.
      p. cm. — (Our fragile planet)
  Includes bibliographical references and index.
  ISBN-13: 978-0-8160-6217-1 (hardcover)
  ISBN-10: 0-8160-6217-X (hardcover)
  1. Land use—Environmental aspects. 2. Nature—Effect of human beings on. 3. Environmental management. 4. Sustainable development. I. Title. II. Series.

  HD108.3.D47 2007
  333.73'13—dc22   2007025453

Text design by Annie O'Donnell
Cover design by Ben Peterson

Printed in the United States of America

Bang NMSG 10 9 8 7 6 5 4 3 2 1

This book is printed on acid-free paper.

Cover photograph: © polartern / Shutterstock.com

Contents

Preface

The planet is a marvelous place: a place with blue skies, wild storms, deep lakes, and rich and diverse ecosystems. The tides ebb and flow, baby animals are born in the spring, and tropical rain forests harbor an astonishing array of life. The Earth sustains living things and provides humans with the resources to maintain a bountiful way of life: water, soil, and nutrients to grow food, and the mineral and energy resources to build and fuel modern society, among many other things.

The physical and biological sciences provide an understanding of the whys and hows of natural phenomena and processes—why the sky is blue and how metals form, for example—and insights into how the many parts are interrelated. Climate is a good example. Among the many influences on the Earth's climate are the circulation patterns of the atmosphere and the oceans, the abundance of plant life, the quantity of various gases in the atmosphere, and even the sizes and shapes of the continents. Clearly, to understand climate it is necessary to have a basic understanding of several scientific fields and to be aware of how these fields are interconnected.

As Earth scientists like to say, the only thing constant about our planet is change. From the ball of dust, gas, and rocks that came together 4.6 billion years ago to the lively and diverse globe that orbits the Sun today, very little about the Earth has remained the same for long. Yet, while change is fundamental, people have altered the environment unlike any other species in Earth's history. Everywhere there are reminders of our presence. A look at the sky might show a sooty cloud or a jet contrail. A look at the sea might reveal plastic refuse, oil, or only a few fish swimming where once they had been countless. The land has been deforested and strip-mined. Rivers and lakes have been polluted. Changing conditions and habitats have caused some plants and animals to expand their populations, while others have become extinct. Even the climate—which for millennia was thought to be beyond human influence—has been shifting due to alterations in the makeup of atmospheric gases brought about by human activities. The planet is changing fast and people are the primary cause.

OUR FRAGILE PLANET is a set of eight books that celebrate the wonders of the world by highlighting the scientific processes behind them. The books also look at the science underlying the tremendous influence humans are having on the environment. The set is divided into volumes based on the large domains on which humans have had an impact: *Atmosphere, Climate, Hydrosphere, Oceans, Geosphere, Biosphere,* and *Polar Regions.* The volume *Humans and the Natural Environment* describes the impact of human activity on the planet and explores ways in which we can live more sustainably.

A core belief expressed in each volume is that to mitigate the impacts humans are having on the Earth, each of us must understand the scientific processes that operate in the natural world. We must understand how human activities disrupt those processes and use that knowledge to predict ways that changes in one system will affect seemingly unrelated systems. These books express the belief that science is the solid ground from which we can reach an agreement on the behavioral changes that we must adopt—both as individuals and as a society—to solve the problems caused by the impact of humans on our fragile planet.

Acknowledgments

I would like to thank, above all, the scientists who have dedicated their lives to the study of the Earth, especially those engaged in the important work of understanding how human activities are impacting the planet. Many thanks to the staff of Facts On File and Chelsea House for their guidance and editing expertise: Frank Darmstadt, Executive Editor; Brian Belval, Senior Editor; and Leigh Ann Cobb, independent developmental editor. Dr. Tobi Zausner located the color images that illustrate our planet's incredible beauty and the harsh reality of the effects human activities are having on it. Thanks also to my agent, Jodie Rhodes, who got me involved in this project.

Family and friends were a great source of support and encouragement as I wrote these books. Special thanks to the May '97 Moms, who provided the virtual water cooler that kept me sane during long days of writing. Cathy Propper was always enthusiastic as I was writing the books, and even more so when they were completed. My mother, Irene Desonie, took great care of me as I wrote for much of June 2006. Mostly importantly, my husband, Miles Orchinik, kept things moving at home when I needed extra writing time and provided love, support, and encouragement when I needed that, too. This book is dedicated to our children, Reed and Maya, who were always loving, and usually patient. I hope these books do a small bit to help people understand how their actions impact the future for all children.

Introduction

Humans are land dwellers; they reside on the rock, sediment, and soil that make up the Earth's geosphere. Although people may fly through the atmosphere in an airplane or spaceship, or glide under the ocean's surface in a submarine, these trips can last for only a limited time and must be taken in a self-contained habitat. Humans may briefly visit other realms, but they live on the land. The land provides the surface for nearly all of human existence. The land supports life and supplies essential resources such as food, fiber, wood, metals, and energy. The land also provides a place for discarding wastes. People have relied on the land and all it provides for all of human existence. Initially, people took the resources the land provided without changing the land much; but, over time, people have increasingly altered landscapes to serve human needs.

The amount of landscape that humans have altered has increased dramatically in recent times for two reasons: There are many more people on Earth than ever before, and many of those people consume more resources at a much higher rate. The human population has grown from 250 million in A.D. 950, to 1 billion in 1818, 2 billion in 1932, 4 billion in 1982, 6 billion in 1999, and nearly 6.6 billion as of 2007 (dates approximate). All of these people need food, water, clothes, and some sort of shelter. In some parts of the world, people have grown accustomed to having much more than that: cars, computers, mobile phones, nice clothes, and a large amount and variety of food. An increasing number of people demanding more material goods means more and more of the Earth's surface is being exploited for human needs. Right now, about 50% of the ice-free land area is used by humans. It is estimated that by 2032, when the human population could be over 8 billion, 70% of that land will be under human influence.

But to say that the land has been altered because human population has grown so dramatically, however true, is a sort of a chicken-and-egg argument. The situation can be described in reverse as well. While humans have altered more of the landscape because of their increased numbers, it could be said that the human population has increased because humans have been so successful at altering the landscape to suit their needs.

Natural landscapes include forest, scrub, prairies, grassland, tundra, and desert. In some circumstances, people use landscapes without altering the natural state. For example, they may hunt deer in a forest or harvest fruit from cacti in a desert. But as more people demand more resources from a landscape, the terrain is more likely to be kept in a natural but altered state. People may log a forest for the timber and then plant a tree farm in its place, with the goal of promoting high timber production. However, many managed forests hardly resemble the original forest ecosystem.

Ultimately, people may entirely alter a landscape, as when they clear a forest and transform it into farmland or a city. Landscapes may also be used for the resources they contain: A mining company will dig mines in an area that is rich in mineral resources, or an energy company will build a wind farm in a mountain pass. Lands may also be considered suitable for disposing various types of waste.

Virtually all of these changes alter the water cycle and local climate and reduce the number of species that live in the landscape. When water is diverted from its natural course to farms, industries, and households, that water is no longer available to sustain the natural landscape. Chopping down a large area of forest also changes the region's climate by making it wetter or, more likely, drier. Changing land use reduces biodiversity. A forest, particularly a tropical rainforest, overflows with many different species of plants and animals. Even grassland contains a wide variety of living things. When these

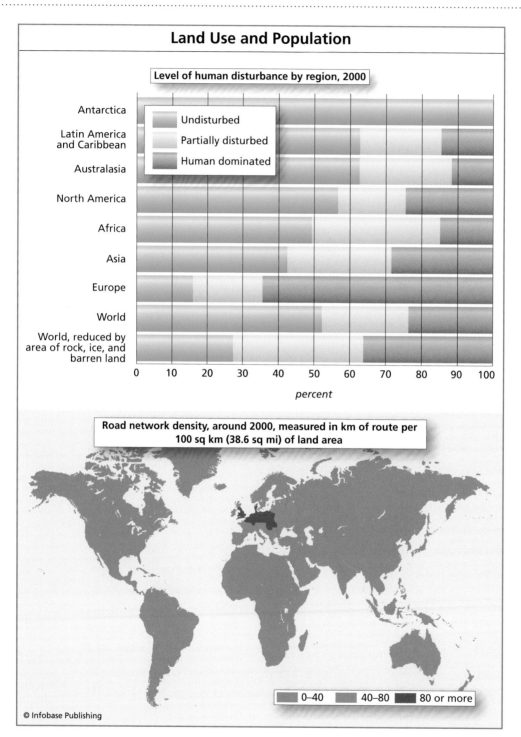

Land Use and Population

Level of human disturbance by region, 2000

Antarctica
Latin America and Caribbean
Australasia
North America
Africa
Asia
Europe
World
World, reduced by area of rock, ice, and barren land

Undisturbed
Partially disturbed
Human dominated

percent

Road network density, around 2000, measured in km of route per 100 sq km (38.6 sq mi) of land area

0–40   40–80   80 or more

© Infobase Publishing

landscapes are replaced by farmland, the number of species in the area dramatically decreases. When they are replaced by a city, the decline in biodiversity is even greater.

As landscapes are altered, the distribution of energy changes dramatically. In natural ecosystems, plants are the primary producers of food. Plant photosynthesis provides food energy to the wide variety of animals and other organisms that depend on them. (In the oceans, plankton are the main primary producers.) In a human-dominated landscape, plants are still the primary producers, but much of the food energy they produce goes directly or indirectly to feeding people. Currently, people use between one-third and one-half of global primary production—energy that is no longer available to support other organisms.

Natural landscapes have built-in systems for cleansing the wastes produced within them: Animal wastes, for example, are broken down by single-celled bacteria to become nutrients. Natural landscapes can process a certain amount of human waste, but they cannot accommodate the magnitude and type of waste that humans now produce. Also, human landscapes are not as good at processing pollutants. Farms, for example, can break down some pollutants, but wetlands can remove even more. As a result of the changes that humans have made to landscapes and the enormous increase in wastes, the water, air, and land have become polluted.

Altering the land from its natural state to agricultural or urban uses has broader consequences. Reducing forest area increases the amount of carbon dioxide (CO_2) that enters the atmosphere. CO_2 is a greenhouse gas, one of the atmospheric gases that trap some of the Earth's heat. Increasing atmospheric greenhouse gases is the major contributor to the increase in worldwide temperatures, a phenomenon

As world population and the global economy have grown, ever more land has been cleared, drained, paved or planted. Road networks not only change the character of the landscape, but they also give people access to previously inaccessible areas.

known as global warming. While most of the increases in atmospheric CO_2 that have occurred since 1850 are the result of fossil fuel use, about 35% may be related to changing land-use practices, such as the replacement of forests by farmland and urban areas.

This volume in the *Our Fragile Planet* series explores how people use the land, how they transform natural landscapes to human land-scapes, and the environmental consequences of changing land use. Each part describes a type of land use: Part One looks at wild lands and forests; Part Two reviews aspects of food production, including the practices of agriculture and the meat industry; Part Three examines mineral resource extraction, its effects, and what happens after mines close; Part Four discusses power generation from both renewable and nonrenewable sources; Part Five reviews the issues of urbanization and its environmental effects; and Part Six examines waste disposal, including both solid and nuclear. Each part looks at how land area is used for these purposes today and considers more environmentally sound ways of using the land. Where possible, this discussion is pre-sented in terms of sustainability: the idea that people living and using the Earth's resources today should not compromise the needs of future generations for the sake of present economic gain.

PART ONE

WILD LANDS AND FORESTS

Land Use and Wild Lands

This chapter comprises four sections: The first section describes the three major rock types, which will become an important part of later topics such as soil development and mining. The different ways that humans have used land in the past and the transitions between those uses are discussed in the second section. The third section discusses the preservation of wild lands, which are lands that are not used but are kept more or less in their original form. The final section describes the concept of **sustainability**.

THE THREE ROCK TYPES

Rocks are made of **minerals**. A mineral is a naturally occurring, inorganic substance with a characteristic chemistry and form. Nearly all rocks are made of minerals, although a very few, such as coal, are not. (Coal is organic and so does not meet the definition for a mineral.) There are three major types of rocks: **igneous**, **sedimentary**, and **metamorphic**. Although igneous and metamorphosed igneous rocks make up most of the Earth's crust, sedimentary rocks form a thin veneer that covers over 75% of the continents.

Igneous rocks crystallize from melted rock known as **magma**. If the magma cools slowly, deep in the Earth's crust, it becomes a **plutonic rock**. However, if the magma erupts from the chamber onto the Earth's surface as lava, it cools into a **volcanic rock**. Because plutonic rocks lie beneath the surface, they cool slowly, which allows the minerals time to form into relatively large crystals. Volcanic rocks that erupt onto the Earth's surface cool rapidly. With little time to form, the mineral crystals in these rocks are extremely small or do not form at all.

Atoms, Molecules, and Chemical Bonding

An **atom** is the smallest unit of an **element** that maintains the properties of that element. An atom's center contains the **nucleus**, which contains **protons**, with a small positive electrical charge, and **neutrons**, with no charge. An atom's **atomic weight** is the sum of its protons and neutrons. A particular element will always have the same number of protons in its nucleus, but it may have a different number of neutrons. For example, the element potassium always has 19 protons, but it can have 20, 21, or 22 neutrons. Therefore, the atomic weight of a potassium nucleus can be 39, 40, or 41, which creates the different **isotopes** of potassium, potassium-39, potassium-40, or potassium-41.

Electrons orbit the nucleus in shells. Each electron has a small negative electrical charge. If the number of protons and electrons in an atom are equal, the atom has no charge. Atoms are most stable when their outer electron shells are full. An atom will give, take, or share one or more electrons to fill or completely empty its outer electron shell to achieve stability. An **ion** is an atom that has gained or lost an electron. If an atom loses an electron, it has lost a negative charge, so it becomes a positive ion, which is called a **cation**. If it gains an electron, it gains a negative charge and becomes a negative ion, which is called an **anion**.

A **molecule** is made up of more than one atom or ion and has no electrical charge. **Chemical bonds** allow ions to come together to form molecules. These bonds arise because unlike charges attract each other.

There are many igneous rock types, depending on the composition of the magma and whether it cools inside or outside the crust. Many kinds of magma are unable to flow to the Earth's surface and therefore cool inside the crust to form **plutons**. The chemical composition of magma also determines how explosive the volcanic eruption that brings it to the surface will be. Magmas that are high in silica (a combination of the elements silicon and oxygen) contain a lot of gas and erupt explosively from a volcano. These silica-rich magmas do not flow easily because they are viscous and most often cool slowly to form plutons such as the granites that make up the Sierra Nevada mountains of California. Silica-poor magmas flow more easily. These types of magma create rivers of lava such as those seen on Kilauea Volcano in Hawaii, which cool to become **basalt** rock.

Sedimentary rocks form from **sediments**—rock and mineral fragments that are compacted or cemented into a solid (clastic sedimentary rocks) or that precipitate from water (chemical sedimentary rocks). Clastic rocks are created from sediments that are deposited in environments such as beaches, dunes, or lakes. If the sediments are buried by other sediments, the overlying weight forces air and fluids from the tiny spaces between them until they become compacted into a rock. Sediments may also be cemented by fluids carrying dissolved minerals that are deposited between the sediment grains. Sandstone is a common clastic sedimentary rock.

Water containing dissolved minerals forms chemical sedimentary rocks if the minerals precipitate, as when seawater evaporates near a shoreline. Animals also precipitate minerals into shells that can later become part of a rock. Carbonates, made mostly of the mineral calcium carbonate (calcite), are the most abundant chemical sedimentary rocks. Calcite is also called lime; limestone is calcite in rock form. **Coal** is an organic sedimentary rock made of the compacted and heated remains of plants and animals.

Any rock that is altered (but not melted) by heat, pressure, or deformation (unequally applied pressure) is a metamorphic rock. The conditions necessary for metamorphism are found inside the

Earth. Heat for metamorphism has two common sources: the heat that is found deep within the Earth or the heat that radiates from a nearby pluton. The pressure comes from being buried beneath sediments and rocks or from deformation caused by the rocks moving (such as during an earthquake). Hot fluids can also cause metamorphism. They can originate as **groundwater**, which is water that is found in soil or rock beneath the ground surface, or they can come from a magma.

The two major types of metamorphism are contact and regional. Rocks close to a pluton undergo contact metamorphism from the heat and fluids that radiate from it. (Marble is limestone that has undergone contact metamorphism.) Regional metamorphism takes place over enormous areas when rocks are exposed to the tremendous temperatures, pressures, and forces found in the Earth's lower crust or upper mantle (the layer beneath the crust). Schist, which contains elongate, plate-like minerals, is a typical rock formed by regional metamorphism.

Any type of rock—igneous, sedimentary, or metamorphic—can be changed into any other type of rock. It can even become a different variety of the same type. Any rock that is melted, maybe by being dragged into the mantle or by experiencing a decrease in its overlying pressure, will crystallize into an igneous rock. A rock that is broken into sediments and deposited can be petrified into a sedimentary rock. Any rock can be altered by heat, pressure, or deformation to become a metamorphic rock. The interconnection of all rock types is referred to as the rock cycle.

THE EVOLUTION OF LAND USE

Throughout much of human history, land was mostly unmodified by human activity. In early days, this **wilderness** was inhabited and used by people but was not significantly altered. Wilderness could be any type of untouched land: forest, prairie, desert, tundra, ice, or scrub. Wilderness can still be found today, but in ever-decreasing areas.

Early humans lived as hunters and gatherers and took what they needed from the land and water nearby. Small groups, usually of extended families, gathered edible plants such as nuts, tubers, seeds, and greens from the environment and hunted and fished. They burned wood for warmth, food, and protection. In some regions, groups moved with the seasons, following blooming plants or migrating herd animals. Some of these groups altered the landscape by burning brush to flush out wildlife and create pasture for game animals. Some experts think that many existing grasslands and prairies are the result of fires set by earlier humans.

Agriculture began about 10,000 years ago in the Zagros Mountains of Iran, although it probably developed independently elsewhere at around the same time. Farming allowed people to create and store a stable food supply and to live in stationary communities. Having a reliable food supply allowed the population density of communities to increase by 10 to 20 times above what they had been in hunter-gatherer times. Natural landscapes, including forests, scrubland, wetlands, and prairies, were converted to farms, depending on the amount of water that was available. The indigenous people of the Amazon rain forest, for example, lived in small groups (as some indigenous people still do today), hunting for meat, collecting fruits and nuts, fishing, and farming root crops. The rain forest easily absorbed these activities with little effect on the **ecosystem**. An ecosystem encompasses all of the plants and animals of a region, including the raw materials that they need to live.

Discovering how to harness a reliable water source initiated the next revolution in human settlement. **Irrigation** began about 6,000 years ago in Ancient Mesopotamia, along the Tigris and Euphrates Rivers. Canals were used to divert water from flowing streams or ponds onto nearby fields. A dam built on a stream creates a lake (or reservoir) behind it, which can also be used as a water source. Irrigation provides water for farming to regions that are too dry or that have pronounced dry seasons. A reliable water source lessens the uncertainty that relying solely on the weather adds to farming. Thanks to irrigation, five

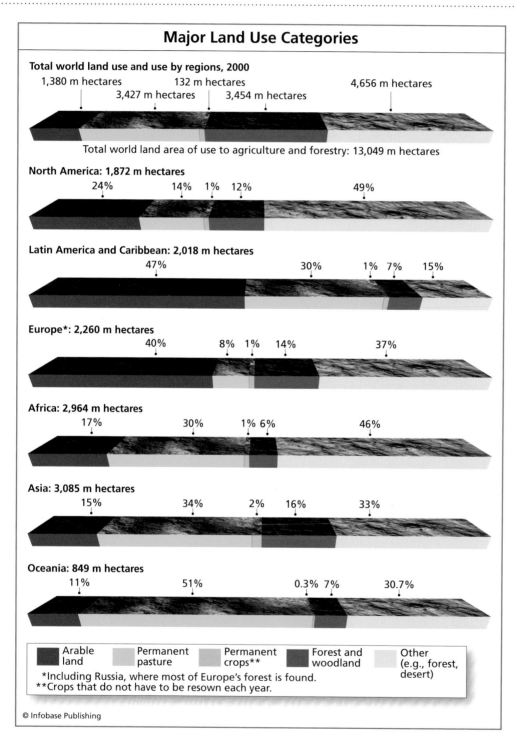

Major Land Use Categories

Total world land use and use by regions, 2000

1,380 m hectares   132 m hectares   4,656 m hectares
      3,427 m hectares   3,454 m hectares

Total world land area of use to agriculture and forestry: 13,049 m hectares

North America: 1,872 m hectares
24%   14% 1% 12%   49%

Latin America and Caribbean: 2,018 m hectares
47%   30%   1% 7%   15%

Europe*: 2,260 m hectares
40%   8% 1% 14%   37%

Africa: 2,964 m hectares
17%   30%   1% 6%   46%

Asia: 3,085 m hectares
15%   34%   2% 16%   33%

Oceania: 849 m hectares
11%   51%   0.3% 7%   30.7%

Arable land | Permanent pasture | Permanent crops** | Forest and woodland | Other (e.g., forest, desert)

*Including Russia, where most of Europe's forest is found.
**Crops that do not have to be resown each year.

© Infobase Publishing

to six times more food can be grown in the same space than with dry farming, in part because many crops can be grown year-round. Even extremely marginal lands, such as deserts, can be made productive by irrigation. Because of irrigation, the abundance of food permitted human populations to further increase and caused the conversion of more natural ecosystems to agricultural landscapes.

The ability to grow more food more easily meant that fewer people were needed to work as farmers. Most people became free to engage in other activities, both economic and cultural, which gave rise to civilization. These people clustered in cities, and transportation networks were established to bring them food, water, and other materials. During the first century A.D., Roman engineers designed, among other modern innovations, huge aqueducts that brought water into the city of Rome from as far as 60 miles (100 kilometers) away. As cities grew, surrounding natural landscapes were converted to farmland to feed the cities, and many farmlands were later converted to urban areas.

Early in human history, economic activities, including agriculture, depended on manual labor. But in the early eighteenth century, mechanization began, and by the late eighteenth and early nineteenth centuries, machinery began to replace people as the main labor source. Crop yields increased, populations grew, and even more people were freed to engage in other pursuits. Coal-powered steam engines ran machinery that could manufacture textiles, build tools, and drive many other devices. In this way, the Industrial Revolution was born. Around 1850, transportation became vastly improved as steam was harnessed to power ships and railways. Later in the nineteenth century, internal-combustion engines and electrical-power generation increased the rate of industrialization and urbanization. With these developments, the Industrial Revolution was in full swing.

A breakdown of land use by category. World land use is shown at top, followed by land use per region. A hectare is the metric equivalent of approximately 2.471 acres.

Each major shift in culture brought about an increase in population and a need for more land to be converted for human use. These shifts also brought about cultural shifts in peoples' lifestyles. Hunter-gatherers could not carry much as they moved in search of food. Therefore, they owned few material goods. By remaining stationary and developing manufacturing and transportation systems that allowed people to move material goods, modern humans have been able to accumulate more and more. An increase in consumer items requires more land to supply the raw materials, more energy to produce them, and more of the environment in which to store the waste.

PRESERVING WILDERNESS

During the nineteenth century, it became clear to people that wilderness was disappearing. From this realization arose a desire to preserve lands of unique beauty or ecological significance. The preservation movement, which first started primarily in the United States and Europe, gave rise to the world's first national park, Yellowstone, in Montana. Established in 1872, Yellowstone is now one of a system of 58 U.S. national parks and has been used worldwide as a model for land preservation.

Governments set aside national parks because they harbor exceptional native organisms and ecosystems, **biodiversity** (the number of different **species** in an ecosystem), or beautiful natural landscapes. These lands are usually protected from development and pollution. Most of them do not permit resources to be taken. Many national parks are popular destinations for recreation and for those who seek relaxation and inspiration. Because many of these parks are heavily used by tourists, they require the construction of hotels, roads, and other services, which impinge on the natural landscape. A few parks, such as Yosemite National Park in California's Sierra Nevada, are virtually "loved to death." A national park designation does not protect parks from problems. Yosemite, particularly the Yosemite Valley, has difficulties with air and water pollution, urbanization, and even such social ills as crime. Everglades National Park is threatened by urbanization, pollution, and falling water levels.

Many other designations for land conservation exist in the United States and around the world. Wilderness areas, for example, are pristine lands where human use is restricted to noninvasive activities such as fishing, hiking, and horseback riding. These regions are often remote and difficult to access. People value wild lands for their recreational, aesthetic, and intellectual value. Because people like to visit them, and because of the money that visitors bring to the area, wilderness areas, as well as national parks, are a positive economic force in a community.

In Alaska, nearly the entire **watershed** of the Noatak River (a watershed consists of a river, all of its tributaries, and the land from which they drain)—more than 6.5 million acres (26,000 square km)—has been set aside as wilderness. Within its superb natural beauty, moose (*Alces alces*), caribou (*Rangifer tarandus*), Dall (bighorn) sheep (*Ovis dalli*), wolves (*Canus lupus*), Canadian lynx (*Lynx canadensis*), grizzly bears (*Ursus arctos horribilis*), and black bears (*Ursus americanus*)

The beautiful scenery of the Strawberry Mountain Wilderness, Malheur National Forest, Oregon. *(Dave Powell / USDA Service)*

roam; and native fish swim in its lakes and streams. Migratory birds hatch their young in this wilderness.

As of May 2007, there were 680 wilderness areas in 44 of the 50 states, preserving 105 million acres (607,000 square km), which totals about 2.5% of the entire United States.

Some lands that are set aside are actively managed for resources such as timber, ranchland, and recreation. The United States Forest Service manages forests and grasslands for multiple uses, primarily logging, ranching, and recreation. The agency manages 300,000 square miles (780,000 square km), an area about the size of the state of Texas. Many managed lands are not preserved as fully functioning natural ecosystems. Some of the forests are largely tree plantations, for example.

Extractive reserves are preserved lands in which resources may be harvested sustainably. In Brazil, where extractive reserves were first created, tropical rain forests are sustainably harvested for rubber, nuts, fruits, and other products.

SUSTAINABILITY

According to the 1987 Brundtland Report, *sustainability* refers to resource use that "meets the needs of the present generation without compromising the ability of future generations to meet their own needs." The 1995 World Summit on Social Development proclaimed that the goal of sustainability was "to achieve a higher quality of life for all people," in which "economic development, social development and environmental protection are interdependent and mutually reinforcing components." These definitions have been broadened as the word has become overused or misused in recent years.

Sustainability can happen on many different levels but is difficult to achieve in total. A forest might produce timber sustainably, but because it has been developed into a tree farm with a very unnatural ecosystem, the original forest ecosystem is not sustainable. Resource use may also be sustainable or unsustainable. **Nonrenewable**

resources are those that cannot be replaced, at least not on human timescales; their use, therefore, is unsustainable. Once depleted, all of the fossil fuel **petroleum** contained on the planet will not be replaced by earth processes for many thousands or millions of years. By contrast, **renewable resources** are those that are replaced on a human timescale. Solar energy, for example, reaches some part of the Earth's surface each day and, coming from the sun, is virtually limitless. This is an example of sustainable energy.

There are many problems that make achieving sustainability difficult in the modern world. One major problem is growth in human population, which now occurs mostly in developing nations, and growth in consumption, which occurs in both the developing and developed nations, although on massively different scales. At present, too many nonrenewable resources are being used, and too much pollution and waste is being created, for society to be considered sustainable. However, small units—a single family, a small community, or even a city—are beginning to work toward sustainability.

In some instances, the tourism industry is moving toward sustainability. This type of tourism, called **ecotourism**, is gaining in popularity. Ecotourists support wild lands and the surrounding communities by paying for park user fees, shelter, food, and local guides. Ecotourism creates jobs for local people and gives them an economic incentive to preserve their local landscapes. By visiting wild lands and hiring local guides to show them around, ecotourists learn about both the natural and cultural resources of the local environment and can become aware of the political, environmental, and social climate of the local and national people. Ecotourists strive for minimal impacts on the environment.

WRAP-UP

Since humans evolved, the world has been converted from an entirely natural landscape to a more and more human landscape. At first, this transformation was extremely slow, and most of the changes had little effect on the planet as a whole. But over the past two millennia, and increasingly in the last few centuries and decades, people have been transforming vast amounts of land from natural to human uses. Some landscapes are useful in their natural state: For example, wilderness may help the economy of a region by attracting tourists. Forests may be logged but then allowed to grow back into forest. Other natural landscapes are transformed into agricultural or urban landscapes and may barely resemble their previous natural state.

Forests

Forests are common worldwide where temperatures are not too extreme and there is enough water to support a large number of trees. This chapter discusses the many types of forest. The type of forest that grows in an area depends on the region's climate. Forest biodiversity varies with forest type. High latitude forests (those nearer the poles) have a much smaller number of plant and animals species than low latitude forests (those nearer the equator). Forests perform a number of services that are crucial for the Earth's living creatures, such as producing food, cycling atmospheric gases, and filtering water.

WEATHERING, EROSION, AND SOILS

Plants cannot grow without good soils. Soils have different characteristics based on a region's climate and the plant species that grow there. Soils form when minerals undergo **weathering**, which is the physical and chemical alteration of a parent rock or its minerals at or near the Earth's surface. Most minerals weather because they formed deep in the Earth under conditions that are very different from those that occur at the surface: Temperatures and pressures are higher deep in the Earth, and there is no water or oxygen. When earth processes drag these minerals up to the surface, they are not stable. They break down when exposed to water, atmospheric gases, sunlight, organisms, and other surface conditions. During weathering, a parent rock is physically broken into sediments or chemically dissolved or altered.

Sediments can form new sedimentary rocks or soils. Water, wind, ice, or gravity transports the sediments from their original location to a new location, a process called **erosion**. When the transporting medium slows or stops, such as when the floodwaters of a stream recede, the sediments are deposited. Over time, these sediments may become sedimentary rocks.

Sometimes the weathered material is not eroded but remains above the parent rock. These rock and mineral fragments are then further altered by water, atmospheric gases, plants, and animals to become soils. Soils are crucial to life on Earth because they trap nutrients and water for plants and provide the stability they need to grow. (**Nutrients** are biologically important elements that are critical to **cell** growth. A cell is the smallest unit in a living organism that is capable of engaging in the essential life processes.) Soils form very slowly and only under the right conditions.

Soils vary a great deal in thickness, organic content, and productivity. A soil's base consists of the large and small rock fragments of the parent rock. The upper layers contain a large amount of organic material from the plants and animals that live at the surface. **Topsoil** is the uppermost layer of the soil. This layer contains partially decomposed organic material called **humus**; broken up leaves, flowers, and other organic material, called **litter**; and weathered bits of sand, silt, and clay. Humus absorbs water, reduces evaporation, provides insulation from excess heat and cold, and supplies nutrients.

Besides organic matter, topsoil is full of living things. One kilogram (2.2 pounds) of fertile topsoil contains 30% by weight of organic matter, including about two trillion **bacteria**, 400 million fungi, 50 million algae, 30 million **protozoa** (simple, single-celled organisms),

Severe soil erosion in a wheat field in Washington State. *(Jack Dykinga / USDA)*

Acidity and pH

Acids are solutions with free positively charged hydrogen ions that are sour to the taste. The **pH** of a substance is a measure of its acidity or alkalinity. The H in pH refers to the free positively charged hydrogen ions. The acidity of a substance is measured on the pH scale. The numbers of the pH scale range from 0 to 14, where 7 is neutral, meaning it is neither acid nor **alkaline**. Numbers higher than 7 are alkaline (also called basic); numbers lower than 7 are acidic. The lowest numbers are the strongest acids; the highest numbers are the strongest bases. The pH scale is logarithmic: A change of one unit equals a tenfold increase or decrease in acidity. Thus, even small changes in pH mean large changes in acidity. If clean rain has a pH of 5.6, rain with a pH of 4.6 is ten times more acidic and 3.6 is 100 times more acidic.

Natural rainfall is slightly acidic, with a pH of about 5.6. The acidity of natural rain is due to the small amount of CO_2 that dissolves in rainwater and forms mild carbonic acid. Strong acids can be harmful enough to burn skin. Strong bases are also harmful.

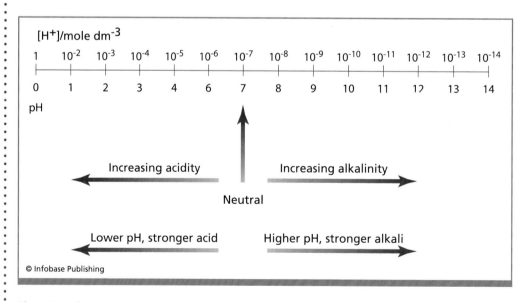

The pH scale. A neutral solution has a pH of 7.0; less than 7.0 is acidic, and greater than 7.0 is alkaline. Hydrogen ion concentration is shown on the upper axis of the scale.

and thousands of insects, worms, nematodes, and mites. Water readily passes through topsoil, taking soluble (or dissolvable) elements to the soil layers below. In all, water, air, and humus account for 1% to 12% of the soil's volume.

Climate is extremely important to soil formation. Soils form faster in warm, wet climates. In humid regions, such as the northeastern United States, where plants are prolific, the topsoil is rich with organic matter. Soils in arid climates, such as the southwestern United States, are thin and contain little organic matter. **Laterite** soils are common in tropical or semitropical climates. These soils are thick but not very fertile; the abundance of rain causes chemical weathering to completely strip the soluble nutrients from the topsoil. Aluminum and iron, which are not soluble, remain in these tropical soils and form **bauxite**, the primary source of the world's aluminum.

Several other factors are important for soil formation. Abundant organic activity increases the amount and rate of soil formation. For example, burrowing animals and plant roots break up soil, add gases, make humus, and form acids that contribute to weathering. Also, the steepness of a slope plays a role in soil formation. On steep slopes, weathered material erodes quickly, resulting in less soil development than on shallower slopes. The direction a slope faces is also important. In the Northern Hemisphere, north-facing slopes receive less light than those that face south. Therefore, vegetation is generally more abundant on south-facing slopes. Time is another factor in soil development. In general, soils mature over time: On average, a soil deepens about one inch (2.5 centimeters) per century.

Soils erode about as rapidly as they form. Although soil is constantly being renewed, it takes 200 to 1,000 years for 1 inch (2.54 cm) to be created, depending on soil type and climate.

FOREST TYPES

Old-growth forests are those that have never been logged or have not been logged for hundreds of years. The high density of trees found in old-growth forests supports many other plants, animals, and microbes. Old-growth forests are very rich ecosystems because they include young trees, old trees, standing dead trees, and decaying logs, all of which provide a myriad of habitats for wildlife. (A **habitat** is the environment in which an organism lives; a habitat is defined by its climate, resource availability, and predators, to name just a few factors). Interestingly, 25% of old-growth forest wildlife depends on snags (trees that are dead but standing) and fallen trees.

Climate determines which of the many types of forests will be found in a region. **Boreal forests** stretch across enormous areas of Canada and northern Eurasia. The growing season is short, and most of the precipitation in this environment falls as snow. Compared to the other forest types, the trees here are short and stand far apart. The dominant trees are firs, with tough, needle-shaped leaves that shed in the winter and can survive frosts. Boreal forests have relatively low species diversity but are home to some beautiful and important animals such as bighorn sheep, Siberian tigers (*Panthera tigris altaica*), Canadian lynx, and moose. Billions of songbirds spend their summers in boreal forests.

Temperate forests extend across the more temperate regions of North America and Eurasia, where the climate is cool, and annual rainfall is high. The two distinct climate types of this region result in two different types of temperate forests. **Deciduous** forests are found where summers are hot and winters are cold. Deciduous trees lose their leaves in the winter so that the leaves do not freeze in the frigid temperatures. Black bears, deer, wolves, foxes, eagles, and small mammals such as squirrels, pine martens (*Marten* sp.), and rabbits (*Lepus* sp.) are common deciduous forest animals. **Evergreen** forests are found where both summers and winters are mild; thus, evergreen trees do not lose their leaves seasonally. Spectacular forests of coastal redwoods (*Sequoia sempervirens*) and Douglas fir (*Pseudotsuga menziesii*), both of which can grow to more than 300 feet (90 meters) tall, are found in western Canada and the United States. These forests support black bears, black-tailed deer (*Odocoileus hemionus columbianus*), and brush rabbits (*Sylvilagus bachmani*) on the forest floor.

Tropical rain forests are more hospitable to life than other forest types: Temperatures are mild and fairly constant year round, and rain is profuse. Because living conditions are so favorable, tropical rain forests support the greatest biodiversity of living organisms on Earth, an estimated 50% to 80% of all species. Plants are at the heart of rain forest biodiversity. Each hectare (2.47 acres, 10,000 square meters) contains 350 to 450 tree species. Biodiversity is so high that only one or two representatives of each tree species are found in each hectare. By contrast, temperate rain forests have between 6 and 30 species per hectare, and three or four species account for almost all trees. Rain forest trees include teak (*Tektona* sp.), rubber trees, (*Hevea brasiliensis*), and many other species. The diversity of plants creates an enormous number of living places for animals; therefore, a tremendous variety of birds, mammals, and reptiles live throughout the forest. Monkeys, apes, jaguars (*Panthera onca*), leopards (*Panthera pardus*), and many other creatures can be found in rain forests. The world's largest rain forest, the Amazon, has the most biodiversity of any ecosystem in the world, with up to 30% of the world's total plant and animal species. Much of the rain forest is remote, and many of these plants and animals are still unknown.

Tropical and subtropical **dry forests** receive a lot of moisture but have up to eight months of drought each year. Because trees lose moisture through their leaves, dry forest trees are deciduous, losing their leaves during the dry season. Compared with rain forests, dry forests have a smaller variety of species, but dry forests also are important locations for biodiversity. Trees in broadleaf dry forests include teak and mountain ebony (*Bauhinia variegata*), which are often logged. Monkeys, large cats, parrots, and ground-dwelling birds are common wildlife.

FOREST ECOSYSTEM SERVICES

Ecosystems and the organisms that live within them provide a number of ecosystem services to the planet. These services keep biological systems—including systems that people rely on—operating. Some important ecosystem services are listed below:

⊕ Nearly all living creatures depend on the ability of plants and other photosynthesizing organisms to create food.

Photosynthesis is the creation of sugar from carbon dioxide and water in the presence of sunlight.

- Insects, birds, and bats carry pollen from one flowering plant to another, contributing to the birth of fertile, healthy plant offspring.
- Bacteria break down plant and animal tissue and release the nutrients contained within so that they are available for reuse by plants.
- Organisms make living spaces for other species. For example, a hole in a tree serves as a home for a woodpecker family.
- Plants keep down soil erosion by holding soil in place with their roots.
- Soils contain minerals, microbes, and plant materials that cleanse the water that trickles through. Soil microbes detoxify or sequester pollutants.
- Living creatures undertake important interactions with the **atmosphere** by cycling or "fixing" atmospheric gases. Plants convert CO_2 into oxygen (O_2) and animals convert O_2 back into CO_2. Although nitrogen is the most abundant gas in the atmosphere, it is not in a chemical form plants can use. Bacteria and algae "fix" the nitrogen—that is, modify it chemically—so that it is useful to plants.
- Plants are an important part of the **water cycle**, which is the movement of water between the oceans, atmosphere, lakes, streams, and organisms. Plants take in water, some of which is evaporated into the atmosphere through a process known as **evapotranspiration**.
- Plants are extremely important for regulating global climate. Plants absorb CO_2, which is an important **greenhouse gas**. Greenhouse gases are crucial for life on Earth: Without these gases, nights would be frigid and days scorching, as on the atmosphere-free Moon. Yet while some greenhouse gases keep the planet's temperature comfortable, excess amounts make the planet warmer. The buildup of greenhouse gases in the atmosphere is the main cause of **global warming**.

Forests contain an enormous plant **biomass**. Biomass is the mass of all the living matter in a given area. Ways in which the biomass of forests is essential are presented below:

⊕ Because they have so many plants, forests are major contributors to evapotranspiration. About 75% of the precipitation that falls on a healthy forest is evaporated back into the atmosphere. Forest plants also absorb water and contribute to the health of soils, which also absorb water.

⊕ The enormous biomass of tropical rain forests plays a major role in containing CO_2. The ecosystem services provided by tropical rain forests have been calculated to be worth $2,000 per hectare per year.

⊕ Some of the water that falls in a forest filters down into groundwater. Forests help recharge groundwater **aquifers**, the layers of underground rock or soil that contain usable water. The top of the water layer—the transition between rock that contains pore spaces filled with air and rock that contains pore spaces filled with water—is called the **water table**.

WRAP-UP

The Earth was once blanketed by a wide variety and enormous extent of forests. As with other ecosystems, early humans used the forests for food, shelter, and other resources. There is evidence that some Native American groups burned forests to create grasslands so that they could hunt more easily. However, most forests remained in their natural state until modern humans found many more uses for forest materials and the land the forests covered. Forests as a whole provide essential services to the Earth, such as containing CO_2, moderating weather, and reducing erosion.

Using Forests

People have long used forests to supply firewood, timber, and other wood products, but rising human population has increased the need for forest products. This chapter discusses **deforestation**. More importantly, rising populations require more food and living space, so more forests are converted to agricultural or urban land. Deforestation changes the local environment by lessening biodiversity and increasing soil loss, flooding, and landslides. On a regional or global scale, forest loss changes weather patterns and allows more carbon dioxide to enter the atmosphere, thereby increasing global temperatures. Many forests are now managed for the crops they produce, such as timber and wood products. These tree farms hardly resemble natural forest ecosystems. However, sustainable forestry practices and reforestation are increasing in popularity in some areas.

DEFORESTATION

Forests are important to human society as sources of timber and wood products such as veneer, plywood, and paper. The trees that

Logging truck piled high with freshly cut logs heads to the mill for processing. *(Sally Scott / iStockphoto)*

supply wood for these products are harvested by logging, which can be done by clear-cutting or selective techniques. Clear-cutting harvests all the trees in a specific area. Temperate forests are commonly clear-cut because many of them contain only a few species, and it is easier and less expensive for all the trees in one spot to be taken together at once. When loggers practice selective logging, they take only the valuable trees from the forest. Selective logging is more common in tropical and subtropical forests, where species diversity is high, and only some of the trees are valuable. Hardwoods such as mahogany are among those trees that are selectively logged from tropical rain forests.

Besides being logged for timber and wood products, forests are also being cleared for agriculture, grazing, and other human activities. Reasons for deforestation include:

- ⊕ Fuel: Half of all downed trees are used for fuel; in developing nations, firewood is often the most economical and easily accessible energy source.
- ⊕ Wood and paper products: At least half of the world's timber and nearly three-quarters of its paper are consumed by 22% of the world's population—people living in the United States, Europe, and Japan. Global paper use has increased sixfold since 1961.
- ⊕ Cattle ranching: Ranchers clear tropical rain forests to create cattle pastures. Some of the beef from these cattle is exported to developed countries, where it becomes fast-food hamburgers and frozen meat products. A quarter-pound hamburger made from cattle grazed in cleared rain forest requires the destruction of about 55 square feet (5.1 square m) of rain forest (the size of a small kitchen).
- ⊕ Agriculture: Forests worldwide are cleared for farmland. The farms supply food and income for the region where they are located.
- ⊕ Resource extraction: Mining, and oil and gas drilling destroy forests. Roads built for access to these resources open up pristine areas for logging, hunting, and other destructive activities.
- ⊕ Industrial development: Pipelines, power lines, roads, dams, and other infrastructure are built to open forests for large-scale industrial development.

The underlying causes of deforestation are economic growth and population growth. Developed nations consume more timber and wood products, while developing nations depend on the income that timber sales from their forests generate. As populations in developing countries rise, more people depend on cleared land for agriculture. Many of these farms are **subsistence farms** where a family can only grow enough food to feed itself and little more. Forests also serve as an outlet for excess human population. For example, the Brazilian government relocated their nation's capital from Rio de Janeiro to Brasilia in 1960 to move people away from the crowded coastline and into the uninhabited interior.

About 80% of the world's old-growth forests are now gone. The temperate forests have been the hardest hit by centuries of logging, especially in Europe and the United States. Britain chopped down nearly all of its virgin forest by about 500 years ago. Mainland Europe's biggest deforestation push came a bit later, during the latter part of the nineteenth century. Deforestation in the United States began with the arrival of the Europeans and continued well into the twentieth century. The nation, once a vast frontier of seemingly limitless trees, now has less than 4% of its original virgin forest. Canada still has enormous tracts of boreal forest and has committed to preserving sizable areas.

With the temperate forests largely logged out, developed nations have increasingly turned to tropical and subtropical forests for wood products. Tropical rain forests once covered as much as 12% of the planet's land surface (6 million square miles [15.5 million sq. km]), but now cover only 5.3% of the Earth's surface (1 million square miles [2.6 million sq. km]). About 120,000 square miles (310,000 sq. km)—an area nearly as large New Mexico, the fifth largest U.S. state—is lost each year, and the rate of destruction is increasing. Projections show that tropical rain forests may be gone in as little as 40 years.

More than half of the planet's remaining tropical rain forest is in the Amazon basin of South America. Much of that is located in Brazil, which has been actively developing its rain forest lands since the 1940s. After the government builds a road into virgin forest, loggers, ranchers, and others move into the area to harvest resources and eventually build communities. Other tropical rain forests are faring just as badly or worse. For example, Malaysia's annual deforestation rate has recently jumped by 85%: 140,200 hectares (1,400 sq. km), which is about 0.65% of Malaysia's forest area, has been lost every year since 2000. In Malaysia and Indonesia, palm oil plantations are responsible for 80% of rain forest loss. The greatest threat to the continued survival of wild orangutans in their native homes (*Pongo pygmaeus* in Borneo and *Pongo abelii* in Sumatra) is rain forest deforestation due to the expansion of palm oil plantations.

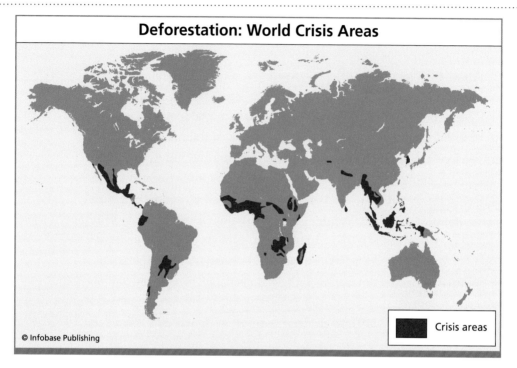

Deforestation: World Crisis Areas

Crisis areas

© Infobase Publishing

Deforestation has become a worldwide cause for concern, especially the removal of tropical forests, which comprise complex and unique ecosystems. The areas most at risk from deforestation are shown in red.

EFFECTS OF DEFORESTATION

Deforestation has many adverse effects. Removing trees decreases a region's biodiversity and also lessens or eliminates the ecosystem services that forests provide. Logging activity degrades not only the logged region but also the areas nearby that are used for access.

The destruction of a forest from clear-cutting is easy to trace. Roads that allow loggers to enter the area are cut through formerly intact forest. Then the loggers remove tree species from an area systematically and completely. Clear-cutting exposes the soil to sunlight, which bakes the soil and kills the **decomposers**, making the soil unhealthy. (Decomposers break down dead plant and animal tissue and waste products into nutrients, which can be used by plants to make food).

Logging requires heavy equipment, the weight of which compacts the soil and makes regrowth difficult.

Selective logging also degrades forests. Heavy equipment moved into the forest to cut down and remove trees damages untargeted plants and churns up the soil, making erosion more likely. When they are cut, falling trees knock down other nearby trees. Selective logging may also cause the valued species to completely disappear locally. A recent satellite study showed that the amount of forest damaged each year by selective logging in portions of the Brazilian Amazon is twice as great as the amount that is clear-cut in those same areas.

The most obvious effect of deforestation is the loss of biodiversity. Species may vanish locally or, if they are found only in that location or have been wiped out in the rest of their range, they may become extinct. A species faces **extinction** when it no longer produces enough young to replace the organisms that die.

When a species is lost, so are its potential benefits for humans. Some plants and animals contain compounds that provide medical benefits for people. Scientists can isolate these compounds and make them into the active ingredients in pharmaceuticals. More than 75% of the top 150 prescription drugs are derived from, or are synthesized to mimic, chemicals that are found in plants, fungi, bacteria, and vertebrates (animals with backbones). One such drug is the important anticancer agent Taxol, which is derived from the Pacific yew tree (*Taxus brevifolia*).

Wild organisms are also used by agriculturalists to improve a characteristic of a domesticated species. To do this, scientists look to wild populations for organisms with the desired trait, find the **gene** that controls it, and breed in or genetically engineer that gene into the domestic population. (A gene is the unit of inheritance that passes a trait from one generation to the next.)

Deforestation reduces or eliminates the forest's ecosystem services. Removing plant biomass lessens photosynthesis, which limits the number of animals the region can support. Eradicating a forest also alters the water cycle in the region. Evapotranspiration is greatly reduced, which can lower the amount of precipitation that falls both in the deforested region and in regions **downwind** (in the direction the wind is blowing) from that area. Rain forest deforestation in one area of northwestern China has resulted in a one-third decrease in annual precipitation in the region.

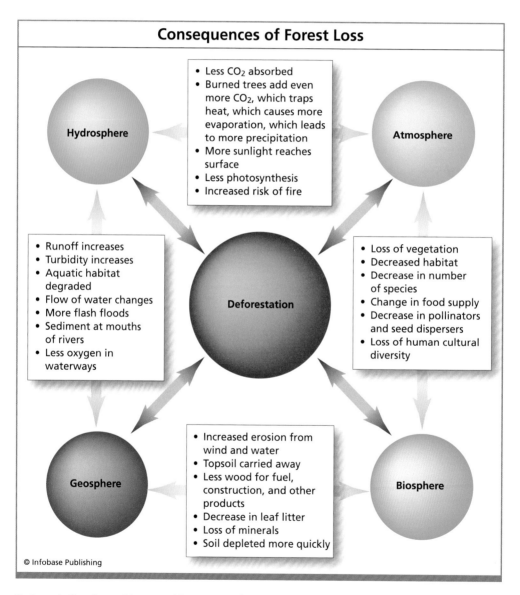

Consequences of Forest Loss

- Less CO_2 absorbed
- Burned trees add even more CO_2, which traps heat, which causes more evaporation, which leads to more precipitation
- More sunlight reaches surface
- Less photosynthesis
- Increased risk of fire

Hydrosphere

Atmosphere

- Runoff increases
- Turbidity increases
- Aquatic habitat degraded
- Flow of water changes
- More flash floods
- Sediment at mouths of rivers
- Less oxygen in waterways

Deforestation

- Loss of vegetation
- Decreased habitat
- Decrease in number of species
- Change in food supply
- Decrease in pollinators and seed dispersers
- Loss of human cultural diversity

- Increased erosion from wind and water
- Topsoil carried away
- Less wood for fuel, construction, and other products
- Decrease in leaf litter
- Loss of minerals
- Soil depleted more quickly

Geosphere

Biosphere

© Infobase Publishing

Deforestation has widespread impact on the health of the planet.

Deforestation increases flooding and erosion. Without forest cover, rainwater runs off the land quickly and causes rivers to swell. One river in the Brazilian Amazon showed a 25% increase in water flow between 1960 and 1995 as agriculture expanded. This river's water carries with it soil and sediments washed away from the vanished forest. A deforested landscape with eroding topsoil loses nutrients at six to eight times the rate of a forested valley, causing long-term deterioration of the soil. The eroded sediments carried by rainwater into the waterways silt up lakes, ponds, man made reservoirs, and even seas and oceans. The sediment clouds the water and hinders photosynthesis in aquatic plants. Its particles may bury plants and animals that live on the lake bottom and clog the animals' feeding apparatus or gills. Entire ecosystems, such as coral reefs, may be buried by sediments. It is estimated that excess sediments due to deforestation have killed 75% of the coral reefs in the Philippines and in the Caribbean Sea off Costa Rica. Australia's Great Barrier Reef receives five to ten times as much sediment as it did before the arrival of Europeans.

Deforested slopes are much more prone to landslides than forested slopes where the trees' roots hold the dirt together. When the soil that is exposed after logging becomes laden with water during a heavy rain, gravity may pull the soil downhill. In February 2006, a massive landslide killed more than 1,000 people and buried portions of the town of Guinsaugon in the Philippines. The region is heavily deforested, and illegal logging was common, even though a logging ban had been initiated more than a decade earlier. Some threatened villages were evacuated in late 2004, but many of the people returned to their homes and livelihoods because they had nowhere to go and no other way to provide for themselves. The massive reforestation effort required to prevent the landslide had been discussed but never implemented.

Cutting down trees means that they are no longer available to absorb carbon dioxide. If, as often happens, the loggers also burn the debris, the plant matter releases its absorbed CO_2 back into the atmosphere. Increases in atmospheric CO_2 levels raise global temperature and contribute to global warming.

Mass Wasting

Mass wasting, which is the downslope movement of rock and soil due to gravity, is the most destructive of erosional forces. On average, mass wasting kills 25 people and causes $1 billion in damages in the United States each year. (The general term for material moving downhill is *landslide*.)

Although gravity continually pulls rock and soil downslope, hillsides ordinarily remain stable. This is because cohesion and friction with other nearby materials keeps them in place.

Some slopes are more prone to landslides than others. Steeper slopes, or those that are made of loose material, are more likely to experience landslides. The removal of the base of a steep or loose slope by stream erosion, wave erosion, or human excavation may cause slope failure. Because plant roots bind soil together, loss of vegetation by fire or logging also contributes to slope failure. And while small amounts of water bind sediment grains together and inhibit landslides, too much water acts as a lubricant and increases the likelihood of slope failure. Water also adds weight to a slope, further increasing its instability. Finally, certain events—an earthquake, a volcanic eruption, or even a loud noise—may trigger a landslide on an already unstable slope.

There are several types of mass wasting. For example, the material may **flow, slide**, or fall down a slope. In flow, loose sediment moves as a viscous (gooey) fluid. Another type, called **creep**, occurs when shallow layers of a soil flow slowly downhill, a phenomenon that is common in humid climates. Although creep is not life threatening—a creeping slope moves at only about one-half inch (1 cm) per year—it can damage hillside property, breaking streets and sidewalks and cracking retaining walls and foundations. Indications of creeping slopes are tree trunks that are curved in the downslope direction and tilted fences, gravestones, or telephone poles. Rapid flows, called **mudflows**, can move at up to 50 miles (80 km) per hour. Mudflows are ordinarily slurries of mud and rocks.

During slides, a large slab of rock or soil moves downhill along fractures. In one type of slide, known as a **slump**, a block of soil slips downhill and rotates backwards into the hill. In the other type of slide, a **rock slide**, chunks of bedrock break up as they slide downhill. Sometimes air becomes compressed beneath the rocks, creating a kind of river that carries them at speeds of up to 300 miles (500 km) per hour. When a rapidly moving rock slide hits the bottom of the slope in a valley, it sometimes travels up the other side. Avalanches of snow and ice are similar to rock slides.

A fall is exactly what it sounds like— a rapid free fall of material that occurs when chunks of rocks break away from cliffs. Falls are generally vertical.

Even where forests are not logged directly, forest ecosystems are damaged by nearby logging. Clear-cutting is often done in patches, so the intact forest remains in fragments surrounded by edges. Dividing large ecosystems into these smaller islands of habitat separated by agriculture or urban land is known as **habitat fragmentation**. Forest edges receive more sunlight and wind and are therefore drier than forest interiors. The additional sunlight increases the growth of low plants such as shrubs. Drier conditions and more small plants increase the intensity of forest fires, which often start during deforestation or in areas of human activity. Forest fires harm the remaining forest ecosystem and nearby developments.

Forest loss also means a loss of aesthetic beauty. In economic terms, beautiful lands may attract tourists, who bring money into the area. Deforestation can lead to economic losses for nearby communities.

FOREST MANAGEMENT

Forests are managed for many purposes. Historically, foresters have been charged with harvesting timber and planting new trees, but modern forests may be managed for ecosystem services as well as for their aesthetic value. Forest management practices include planting, protecting, thinning, controlled burning, felling, extracting, and timber processing.

The most extreme type of managed forest is a tree farm, which is also called a plantation. Tree farms are **monocultures**, where only one species of tree is grown. Little attempt is made to grow native trees, and the species chosen for planting is usually resilient and fast growing. Pine (*Pinus* sp.), spruce (*Picea* sp.), and eucalyptus (*Eucalyptus* sp.) are common, as are hybrids between two species or trees that are genetically modified. Farmers maximize the conditions that lead to easily harvested good timber and wood products. They grow the trees as they might any crop, planting them all at the same time and in rows, for example. Rather than being allowed to mature, the trees are harvested after 10 to 60 years. Decaying dead wood, which is very important to natural forest ecosystems, is absent.

A Patula pine plantation (*Pinus patula*) near Pietermaritzburg, South Africa. *(Paul Bolstad / University of Minnesota / www.forestryimages.org)*

Because the trees are often not native to the area, and because they are all the same size, they are not good habitat for local animals. A tree farm does not much resemble a natural forest ecosystem. At this time, forest plantations make up less than 5% of the total forested area worldwide but account for 20% of current wood production. In Finland, for example, forests are completely managed as plantations by the wood products industries. In contrast, in parts of Canada, when trees are cut, new trees are planted in the forest ecosystem and allowed to grow wild.

Forest managers may plant trees in a tree farm, or they may create a natural forest where one no longer exists. Reforestation supplies trees to the timber industry and increases the amount of forest ecosystem. If the soil is healthy, and other conditions are favorable, reforestation can take place with no human effort. For example, temperate forests in the eastern United States readily reestablish themselves in any location where the trees are not prevented from growing.

If the soil has been degraded, more active reforestation efforts are necessary. Soil degradation occurs in arid regions, where the soil becomes too dry; in land that has been extensively grazed, so that the soil is compacted; in tropical areas, where the soil may form a crust that prevents water from penetrating; or in any area where erosion has removed too much topsoil. In these instances, people may break up the soil or add soil, plant seedlings, add water, or build protection from erosion. If the planted forest has many species that become well established, with time other organisms will move in, and the biodiversity level of the ecosystem may approach that of the original forest.

Companies in some Central American countries, such as Costa Rica and Panama, are planting trees for future lumber harvests on old cattle pastures. Slow-growing trees such as teak and mahogany are being planted so that they will be ready for the market after the natural Asian forests (which are the world's current source of many rain forest woods) disappear. Faster-growing trees, such as pine and eucalyptus, are also planted. These farms typically have several species mixed; thus, they resemble a forest more than a plantation. These forests restore the soil, support local plants and animals, and remove CO_2 from the atmosphere.

Forest management has long meant fire suppression. Forest fires were thought to damage trees and forest ecosystems. Yet, in the types of forests in which fire is a natural part of the ecosystem, such as boreal and temperate forests (but not tropical rain forests or dry forests), fire suppression usually means the forest ecosystem is unhealthy. These forest ecosystems need fires to clear out brush and germinate seeds. Fire suppression causes too much brush to accumulate, so that the delayed (and inevitable) fire will burn hotter. The excess fuel allows the fire to travel up the tree trunks, damaging leaves and wood. An intense fire may even burn the organic portion of the topsoil, making recovery of the ecosystem difficult. In many regions today, forest management strategies include controlled burning to keep down the accumulation of fuel.

SUSTAINABLE FORESTRY

The goal of some foresters, particularly in Europe and North America, is to manage forests sustainably. Sustainable forestry practices are meant to mimic natural processes as much as possible because these are the conditions in which the trees evolved. Forests that contain all stages of tree growth and the right amount of woody underbrush more closely resemble natural ecosystems and make better homes for forest animals. The idea is that healthier forests contain healthier trees so that those that are logged yield more—and higher quality—wood.

To know what a particular forest's natural processes are, forest managers use the same type of old-growth forest as a guide. In a sustainable forest, only as much timber is removed as the forest can grow back without damage to the soils, the watershed, or the seed source. In many forests, that means no more than 25% to 35% of the trees can be harvested, although this number varies depending on the forest type.

Selective logging, for example, mimics a tree falling down. Trees to be logged are carefully chosen with regard to the space between them and the amount of underbrush that grows in their vicinity. However, some foresters, particularly in boreal forests, consider clear-cutting to be sustainable because a clear-cut area resembles land that is cleared by a natural forest fire. But environmentalists and some forest managers argue that clear-cutting reduces the forest's biodiversity.

In sustainable forestry practices, old-growth forests also serve as a source of seeds. Old trees are more resilient and better adapted to their environment and likely produce better offspring than trees that were killed off by disease or fire. (An **adaptation** is a structure or behavior alteration that is able to be passed from one generation to the next.) Selective logging practices that take all the best trees while leaving the weakest trees behind to serve as the seed source are to be avoided.

Other common practices for managing sustainable forests include controlled burning, a common and important practice in boreal and temperate forests. To combat some of the problems caused by fragmentation, managers connect forest fragments with corridors of native habitat so that animals and even pollen can travel between them.

In recent years, consumers have started a demand for wood products from sustainably managed forests. Certification programs inform customers whether a wood product comes from a sustainably managed forest. There are several certification systems, each with its own certification criteria. The Forestry Stewardship Council (FSC) is considered to be very reliable. As of December 2006, the FSC had certified more than 200 million acres (809,400 sq. km) of forest in 76 countries as sustainably managed. About 47% of these forests were in Europe, 32% in North America, 11% in Central and South America, 7% in Asia and Oceania, and 3% in Africa. Becoming certified is difficult for developing nations because they do not have the money or political clout to follow sustainable practices.

A forest may also be managed for reasons other than timber and wood products. The Area de Conservación Guanacaste (ACG) in northwestern Costa Rica is a sustainable forest that is being managed for its socially useful "crops." In addition to the forest's aesthetic beauty and scientific value, the crops are ecotourism, biological education (for local children and Costa Rican and international researchers), biodiversity services (pharmaceuticals and other products), and ecosystem services (sequestering CO_2). AGC scientists are also restoring tropical dry forest, one of the most threatened forest ecosystems, by buying and converting ranchland. The idea is that if the AGC provides useful services and jobs, the local people will want to keep it as forest rather than convert it to ranchland.

WRAP-UP

One major "use" of land is as forests. While some forests are allowed to remain as natural ecosystems, trees are increasingly grown as crops, as they are in areas of Europe where virgin forests were logged centuries ago. In the United States, little remains of the once vast expanses of virgin forests. Some forests have been replaced with managed plantations, which resemble natural forests to varying degrees. Tropical rain forests in developing nations are now being logged for wood and wood products for the developed nations. Increasingly, though, people are gaining awareness that forests are valuable ecosystems, which is leading to sustainable forest management. Sustainable forests can both produce timber and exist as viable ecosystems for the indefinite future.

PART TWO

FOOD PRODUCTION

Agriculture

Forests are often cleared to make way for farms and ranches, which now cover about the same amount of the Earth's surface as forest, about 40%. This chapter covers how, in the past 40 years, cropland has increased approximately 12%, while grain harvests have almost doubled. These increases in production are the result of the **Green Revolution**—advanced agricultural technologies that primarily involve changes to grain strains, but that also include mechanization, irrigation, and the widespread use of chemical pesticides and fertilizers.

CREATING AGRICULTURAL LAND

People have cleared wild lands for farms since the beginning of agriculture. Lands that are suitable for farming are called **arable**. Arable lands have nutrient-rich soil and at least some water available. In the developed countries, most of the arable lands are already being farmed. Among these are most of the lands once covered by the deciduous forests of Europe and the eastern United States. The former grasslands of the midwestern United States, with their rich soils, are now extensively farmed and grazed by domesticated animals. Wetlands have been drained to create highly productive farmlands. **Floodplains**, which have typically been important locations for farms because of the annual floods that bring nutrients to the soil, have long been used for agriculture. In many locations, the small agricultural communities that took advantage of the fertile floodplains have grown into modern cities.

In the developing nations that mostly lie within tropical and subtropical regions, rain forests are increasingly being cleared for farmland. Peasant farmers prepare the land by slashing down trees at the forest edge, then burning the unusable scrub and other material. This type of farming is called **slash-and-burn agriculture**. However, former rain forests make terrible farmland because of their nutrient-poor laterite soils. In a few years, the soil is exhausted of nutrients, and peasants graze cattle on it. The cattle then tramp down the soil, leaving behind a bricklike surface layer. Meanwhile, the farmers must slash and burn a new plot at the forest's edge. Large plantations are more successful at growing crops on former rain forest land because plantation owners (who are often corporations) can afford to use fertilizer to replenish the soil. Crops grown on land that has been slashed and burned include sugarcane, bananas, pineapples, peppers, strawberries, cotton, tea, coffee, marijuana, and coca (for making cocaine).

EARLY DEVELOPMENT OF AGRICULTURE

Anthropologists think that the **carrying capacity** of humans on Earth without using agriculture—that is, living as hunters and gatherers—is around 10 million, a number that was reached about 10,000 years ago. (Carrying capacity is the number of organisms that can be sustained indefinitely by an environment.) In a natural system, when the population of a species of animal gets too high, that animal will starve until its numbers align with the amount of available food. Since the beginning of agriculture, people have exceeded the planet's natural carrying capacity because each improvement in farming techniques allows the number of people on Earth to increase.

Most traditional agriculture, including much of the world's agricultural production today, is by subsistence farming. Water for this kind of farming comes from rain or from local irrigation, while supplementary soil nutrients are provided by natural fertilizers, such as animal manure. When conditions are good, a farmer might be able to sell some crops to raise money for supplies; but when conditions are bad, the farmer's family may go hungry. For centuries, subsistence farmers have used water and soil nutrients carefully to protect the ability of the land to produce food for their future.

The development of farming allowed for a steadier, more abundant food supply; as a result, populations increased. Farmers came together to form settlements in places where soil was rich, such as on floodplains, former wetlands, or cleared temperate forests. Settling in one place allowed people to build houses and develop more advanced farming tools, such as simple plows. In some locations, animals such

A subsistence farmer at Gyeongju in South Korea plowing the land by hand.
(Steve Geer / iStockphoto)

as oxen were domesticated and bred for work, relieving the people of some of the backbreaking labor that comes with farming.

At the beginning of the nineteenth century, family farmers still used these age-old techniques. To keep the soil healthy, farmers used crop rotation, crop mixing, and organic fertilizers. Toxic compounds made from tobacco or chrysanthemum leaves were sometimes used as natural pesticides to kill or deter unwanted insects. In developed nations, mechanization, such as the use of the steel plow designed by John Deere, became widespread after 1850. New fertilizers, which included the nutrients nitrates and phosphates, were discovered and gained widespread use. More complex irrigation systems were developed. Mechanization and artificial fertilizers increased the amount of arable land and decreased the number of farmers who were needed for agriculture. In many locations, small family farms were replaced by larger farms or plantations. During colonial times, European-style plantations took over family farms in parts of the developing world. With fewer people needed for farming, large segments of the population were available for other commercial activities, such as factory work. The development of refrigeration and the spread of transportation networks allowed food to be moved from where it was grown to the urban areas that were developing far away from farms. This trend continued as the steam engines of the nineteenth century gave way to the internal-combustion engines of the twentieth century.

At the end of World War II, chemical fertilizers, which were manufactured from the same materials that went into explosives, became even more widespread in the developed nations. At the same time, chemical pesticides and herbicides entered widespread use to keep unwanted pests and plants away from the new industrialized farms. These technological advances brought about the Green Revolution in agriculture.

THE GREEN REVOLUTION

Like other major developments in agriculture, the Green Revolution changed the course of human history. The philosophy of the Green Revolution was to use high-yield crops, ample irrigation water, and

Irrigation in a corn field in Oklahoma. *(Oklahoma Farm Bureau)*

advanced mechanization to feed the maximum number of people as inexpensively as possible. The father of the Green Revolution was Norman Borlaug (1914–), a plant geneticist who received the Nobel Peace Prize for his work in 1970.

Early in his career, Borlaug spent years developing a high-yield, semidwarf (because shorter stalks are less likely to bend over), disease-resistant variety of wheat in Mexico. He did this by **selective breeding**: breeding generation after generation of only the wheat plants that exhibited the traits he desired. His wheat strain increased Mexico's crop sixfold between 1944 (the year Borlaug began his project) and 1963, when the country became a net grain exporter. Borlaug then focused his efforts on India and Pakistan, where a war had brought famine and starvation. There, the importation of his hybrid wheat increased the yields many times. Since the 1960s, both India and Pakistan have increased food production faster than their rapidly expanding populations have grown.

Borlaug's amazing improvements in crop yields have been accompanied by other advances in agriculture. In all, these improvements are:

- ⊕ Crops: People have bred food crops for certain traits—high yield, ease of harvesting and packing, storage longevity, and other traits—over many generations. As a result, now two-thirds of agricultural production is in rice, wheat, and corn—crops that best exhibit these traits. These plants have been bred for these traits for so long that they no longer resemble their wild ancestors. In some developed countries, such as the United States, crops developed by selective breeding techniques are now being replaced by genetically modified crops, where scientists take a gene from one organism and put it into the DNA of another. In this way, crops can be made insect resistant, disease resistant, or more nutritious.

- ⊕ Irrigation: About 70% of the freshwater used annually by humans is for agriculture. (In the United States, the amount is about 41%.) Water for farming can come from surface or groundwater sources. In the past several decades, enormous dams have been built on many of the world's large rivers to provide a reliable water supply for agricultural and urban areas. One side effect of dams is that they keep rivers from flooding (except in extreme instances). Although dams protect homes and businesses in riverside communities, the loss of annual floods from their construction also stops the supply of nutrients to floodplains, so that farmers must use more fertilizers.

- ⊕ Mechanization: Nearly every aspect of agricultural work is now done by machines in developed nations. Tractors are large and efficient. Self-propelled units spray fertilizers, pick crops, and bale hay, among other labor-intensive tasks. All of these labor-saving machines require the heavy use of **fossil fuels**—ancient plants that Earth processes have transformed into oil, gas, or coal.

⊕ Fertilizers: Chemical fertilizers, such as ammonium nitrate and potassium sulfate, are designed to add nutrients and, in some cases, trace elements to the soil. These fertilizers are essential because modern agricultural practices (such as monocultures that are planted year after year and flood control) deplete the soil of nutrients or prevent the addition of nutrients to the soil by flooding. Nearly all chemical fertilizers are produced from mineral deposits. Phosphates are mined from phosphate beds in sedimentary rocks and are chemically altered to forms that are more concentrated and soluble (such as superphosphate, triple superphosphate, or ammonium phosphate). Nitrogen fertilizer is made from atmospheric nitrogen in a process that uses **methane** derived from fossil fuels. (Methane, a **hydrocarbon** gas composed of hydrogen and carbon, is also a greenhouse gas.) Chemical fertilizers are extremely effective. As a result, the past 40 years have seen a 700% increase in their use. In 1950, fewer than 50% of cornfields in the United States received any inorganic nitrogen. Today, that number is above 99%. During that same time, less than 2% of the nitrogen applied to fields in China was from inorganic sources, but now that number is more than 75%.

⊕ Chemical insecticides and herbicides: Herbicides are pesticides used to kill unwanted plants. The best of them selectively kill weeds and leave the crop plant unharmed. Insecticides kill unwanted insects. Chemical insecticides were first used in the early 1940s and became increasingly common in the years after World War II. These chemicals are sprayed over crops by machinery on the field or from the sky by airplanes known as crop dusters.

The Green Revolution has allowed food production to keep pace with population growth. Norman Borlaug's work has been credited with feeding an estimated 1 billion people who likely would otherwise have gone hungry. It has been estimated that 40% of the people alive today owe their lives to ammonium fertilizers. Borlaug maintains that if pre–Green Revolution agricultural techniques were still used, either world population would need to be smaller or much more forestland would need to be converted to farmland. For example, some experts contend that Borlaug's high-yield grain saved 100 million acres (400,000 sq. km) of land in India from conversion to farmland—more than 13% of that country's total area.

WRAP-UP

Despite the obvious successes of the Green Revolution, many of the Earth's people live in dire poverty, with just enough food to eat to survive. When conditions are less than favorable—when there is a drought or a war—mass starvation strikes, particularly in sub-Saharan Africa. Although the Green Revolution gets an enormous amount of credit for saving lives, Norman Borlaug is the first to admit that the Green Revolution has not created a utopia and that there is much more to do to feed people, particularly as global population continues to increase.

The Costs of Modern Agriculture

While no one argues that the Green Revolution has been effective, not everyone believes that it has been wise. The Green Revolution has come at enormous costs to the social structure of many societies and to the environment in such forms as soil degradation, pollution, and loss of natural ecosystems. In his article "The Oil We Eat," in *Harpers Magazine* in 2004, author Richard Manning says, "With the possible exception of the domestication of wheat, the green revolution is the worst thing that has ever happened to the planet." His condemnation of modern agriculture is based on observations of both the social and environmental effects of modern agriculture in the developing and the developed world. The consequences arising from the Green Revolution are the subject of this chapter.

SOCIAL COSTS

Manning and others say that, socially, modern agriculture has torn people's lives apart. Until recently, most people in the developing world lived in rural areas, working as subsistence farmers. Without the ability to buy grain strains, machines, and chemicals—and unable to compete with the corporations and plantation owners who can—these farmers can no longer support themselves. As a result, they have flooded into the cities looking for work; but when they get there, they find that there are few jobs. Most of these people wind up living in abject poverty. It is in the slums of impoverished cities where most of the world's population growth takes place.

ENVIRONMENTAL COSTS

Besides social and economic costs, there are numerous environmental costs arising from the practices of modern agriculture.

Crops

Modern farming practices favor the growth of just a few strains of hybridized or genetically engineered crops. It is easier to grow a single strain of wheat in a field, for example, because planting, growing, and harvesting it use the same techniques and equipment. However, monoculture farming is also vulnerable: A new pest or disease may attack the plant strain and cause considerable damage. Monocultures also result in a loss of pollinators, especially bees, because there is no food for them. The loss of pollinators has deadly consequences for the natural world and could be a problem for agriculture if a particular pollinator is needed for future crops. Monocultures have far less biodiversity than exists on family farms, where multiple species of plants and animals may live together.

In a monoculture, all plants other than the desired crop are considered weeds. Yet some of the weeds are food plants that local people have eaten for centuries. Eliminating backup plants could be setting society up for massive and long-term food shortages if the favored strains become unsuitable for future conditions (for example, due to global warming). Also, as other plant varieties are lost, they are no longer available to be mined for valuable genes that can be used to create new genetically modified crops.

The Environmental Costs of Modern Agriculture

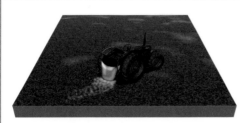

Mechanized farming with heavy use of fertilizer, using finite fossil fuels and generating pollution and CO_2

Intensive use of chemicals to control resistant pests

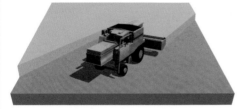

Monocrop cultivation, leading to loss of diversity

Deforestation, leading to shortages of wood for fuel

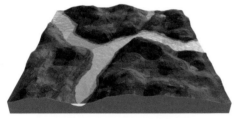

Demands on water resources for irrigation, which can destroy soil by salinization

Overcropping, overgrazing, leading to soil erosion

Population growth, leading to smaller plots and more intensive farming

Loss of plant and animal genetic diversity caused by large-scale farming

The environmental costs of modern agriculture include massive soil erosion, deforestation, pollution, and the loss of plant and animal genetic diversity.

Genetic Homelands of Major Food Groups

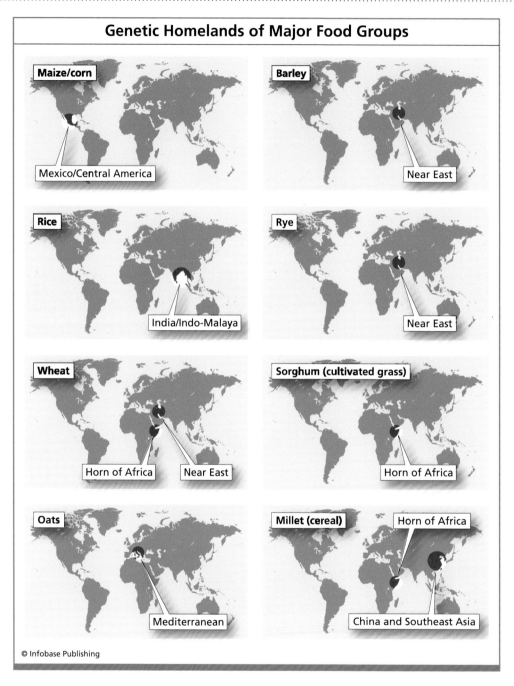

© Infobase Publishing

Of the 270,000 known plant species, only 7,000 have ever been cultivated for food.
Of those 7,000, only 120 are widely cultivated today.

Irrigation

The dependence of modern farming on irrigation requires massive engineering projects, such as dams, to trap and move the water. A dam causes water to flood a valley or canyon upstream, altering the area's ecological and aesthetic qualities and submerging any cultural artifacts that may be there. The water that flows out of the dam is different from the water that flows into it in terms of flow rate, temperature, and the amount of sediment it carries. The river system downstream from the dam is no longer hospitable to native organisms, and the ecology of the area changes. (Ecology is the study of the distribution and abundance of species and their relationship to their environments.) Dams block the upstream migration of fish so that many of them die without reproducing. For example, fisheries in the Nile Delta of Egypt that once supported over a million people have been wiped out by the Aswan Dam.

Dams effectively limit floods, which protects riverside developments. But dams also stop those same floods from depositing nutrients onto a river's floodplain, making fertilizers necessary in places where they were never used before. When the Aswan Dam stopped the Nile River's springtime flooding, soil nutrients were no longer replaced each year, and the soil lost its fertility. To compensate, farmers were forced to add artificial fertilizers. Unfortunately, these fertilizers were too expensive for many of the subsistence farmers of the Nile Valley.

Rivers in arid regions are often overused by people in the region's farms and cities. Overuse causes many desert rivers to run dry during part of the year, bringing about ecological changes, including the loss of native species. For example, the Colorado River, which runs through the southwestern United States and northwestern Mexico, once supported a thriving marshland at the head of the Gulf of California. That wetland is now shrinking and desiccating.

In semiarid and arid regions, enormous quantities of water evaporate from reservoirs and canals, leaving behind salts. The brackish water used to irrigate crops either evaporates or is absorbed by the plants while the salts collect in the soil. If the cropland is poorly drained, enough salts

The Hoover Dam on the Arizona-Nevada border blocks the flow of the Colorado River to create Lake Mead. The dam was built to control floods, improve navigation, and regulate water flow, and the dam's power plant was built to generate electricity. *(U.S. Department of the Interior / United States Bureau of Reclamation)*

collect to produce **salinization** (the overloading of salt) of the farmland. Too much salt in the soil keeps plants from absorbing soil moisture, with the result that the farmland eventually becomes unusable.

Worldwide, salinization has damaged 170,000 square miles (450,000 sq. km) of agricultural land, approximately 20% of the total irrigated land. Approximately 5,800 square miles (15,000 sq. km) of arable land are lost each year, totaling about $11 billion annually in lost production. Portions of the western United States are damaged by salinization, as are lands in the Indus basin of Pakistan, the Tigris-Euphrates region, the Nile basin and many other arid region rivers.

Salinization can be treated by flooding and draining the fields, but only if there is enough water, which may not always be the case. The effects of excess salinization can also be prevented by the use of humic acids, which remove salts from the root regions of plants.

Groundwater is an abundant, year-round water source. Farmers can drill a well into the ground to tap into this underground water supply. In some places, of course, the cost of drilling a well is prohibitive. Overuse of an aquifer causes the water table to fall and wells to run dry. The solution to the problem is to drill deeper, an expensive and sometimes difficult task. Groundwater use in most places far exceeds the rate the water in the acquifer is replenished. The Ogallala aquifer, which provides much of the water for the midwestern United States breadbasket, is being pumped at eight times the rate that it is being recharged. In some areas, the water table is dropping as much as 3 to 5 feet (90 to 150 cm) per year.

Mechanization and Fossil Fuels

Modern farming is entirely mechanized. The machines it depends on are built and powered by the use of natural resources, such as **metals** and fossil fuels. Fossil fuels have many uses in modern agriculture: One acre (4,047 sq. m) of land requires 50 or even 100 times the amount of fossil fuels required for the same acre farmed with traditional methods. Oil is needed for running machinery, manufacturing inorganic fertilizers and pesticides, pumping in water, raising livestock, drying crops, and transporting goods. Between 1945 and 1994, there was a 300% increase in the amount of food grown but a 400% increase in the amount of energy used for agriculture. Since 1994, rates of energy use have increased, but the increase in food production has been minimal. Currently, 17% of the energy consumed annually in the United States is for agriculture.

Increasing the amount of fossil fuel used to grow crops increases the nation's oil deficit because the United States is not self-sufficient in oil. This dependence on imported fossil fuels is a source of instability for the nation's food supply because political situations and prices in the rest of the world are always unpredictable. Fossil-fuel use also has environmental costs, such as air and water pollution and greenhouse gas production.

Fertilizers

High-yield crops need more nutrients to grow than traditional crops—nutrients that are supplied by synthetic fertilizers, such as those made with phosphate. Phosphate mining, from sedimentary rocks or bird guano (excrement), can be ecologically damaging. The tiny South Pacific country of Nauru, for example, has become an environmental wasteland due to the intensive mining of its phosphate deposits.

Most chemical fertilizers are produced from petroleum products. As Richard Manning stated in *Harpers Magazine*,

> Oil is annual **primary productivity** stored as hydrocarbons, a trust fund of sorts, built up over many thousands of years. On average, it takes 5.5 gallons (21 liters) of fossil energy to restore a year's worth of lost fertility to an acre of eroded land—in 1997 we burned through more than 400 years' worth of ancient fossilized productivity, most of it from someplace else.

There are limits to the amount of fossil fuels that are readily available, and using them to grow food has political implications and environmental costs, as described here and in Chapter 11.

The use of inorganic fertilizer can cause extreme damage to aquatic ecosystems. When more fertilizer is placed on a field than the plants can use, the excess runs off into the water supply, where it becomes fertilizer for algae and other aquatic plants. The algae and plants bloom explosively; but when they die, as they inevitably do, the bacteria population increases dramatically to consume the tissue. The numbers of bacteria may become so enormous that the tiny organisms use up all the oxygen in the lake's or sea's water, a state called **eutrophication**. Without oxygen, fish and other animals cannot survive. The oxygen-poor waters become **dead zones**, regions that are hostile to most forms of life.

There are dead zones in nearly all coastal areas where rivers bring excess nutrients into the sea. One of the largest and most persistent in United States coastal waters is in the Gulf of Mexico, off the coast of Louisiana. The Gulf of Mexico dead zone is caused by excess fertilizers brought by the Mississippi River, which drains 41% of the land surface of the United States, an area that includes the rich farmland of the Midwest. Spring rains wash these excess fertilizers from the fields into the river. Surplus nutrients also come from animal manure, golf courses (a golf course uses five times the concentration of fertilizers as a farm), urban lawns (which use twice the fertilizer concentration of farms), and water-treatment plants. The dead zone forms when the excess nutrients reach the Gulf and disappears in the autumn when storms mix the oxygen-poor waters with oxygen-rich waters. In the summer of 2002, the Gulf dead zone grew to its largest area to date, totaling 9,650 square miles (25,000 sq. km), an area slightly larger than the size of Vermont.

Although the dead zone varies in size and duration from year to year, over the past two decades it has continued to appear earlier and become larger. This growth is not surprising because three times more fertilizer runs downstream now than during the period from the 1950s to the 1970s. Flood protection has also contributed to the nutrient problem. Before the construction of the elaborate system of levees along the Mississippi, floodwaters ran over riverbanks and dumped excess nutrients onto the floodplain. Because of the levee system, the nutrients now stay in the river and drain into the Gulf.

Researchers suggest that a 40% to 45% annual cutback in nitrogen use in the Mississippi River drainage area is necessary to shrink the dead zone to 3,000 square miles (5,000 sq. km). Nutrient **runoff** into the Gulf of Mexico can be reduced by requiring farmers to decrease fertilizer use. But, so far, the government requires only voluntary reductions. Researchers also suggest that nutrient levels entering the Gulf can be reduced by reducing runoff. Crops that cover the ground year round rather than only part of the year reduce runoff, as does controlling drainage. Farmers can create marshes around their fields and pump nitrate-rich water through them so that the nitrates can be broken down by bacteria. As a side benefit, such marshes are good environments for fish and water birds.

The fate of the dead zone is important because the Gulf provides 70% of the shrimp and two-thirds of the oysters harvested in the nation each year. The controversy surrounding the control of nutrient runoff pits fishers—the people who are most affected by the dead zone—against farmers, who are the ones most responsible for controlling the problem.

Excess nitrogen can also become part of a chemical reaction that produces acids, a process known as acidification. This contributes to **acid rain**, which decreases the pH of stream and lake water and damages or destroys aquatic ecosystems. Acid rain, primarily the result of coal burning, is considerably more acidic than normal rainwater, which has a pH of around 5.6.

Chemical Pesticides

Monocultures are especially vulnerable to insect pests. If a new insect species enters an area that is covered by a single crop, the organisms will have unlimited amounts of food available to them. If the insect has no natural predators, the pest's population will increase greatly. This means that pests can get out of control. Getting rid of them often requires the use of chemical pesticides. Unfortunately, insects breed quickly and may develop resistance to a chemical, which will mean increasing amounts must be applied.

Chemical pesticides are members of a class of chemicals known as **persistent organic pollutants** (POPs). POPs do not break down or dissipate in the environment, and most of them **bioaccumulate**. Bioaccumulation occurs when animals store in their bodies—primarily in their fat—the entire amount of a chemical that they consume during their lifetimes. Large predators at the top of the food chain accumulate the most. If an animal metabolizes the fat, as happens during lean times, the toxic compound enters the animal's system.

A few POPs are suspected **carcinogens** (cancer-causing agents). Some POPs may cause neurological or other physiological disorders. Of most concern to researchers now is the fact that many of these chemicals are **endocrine disruptors**. These chemicals interfere with the functioning of the **endocrine system**, the system that regulates many of the body's functions, including growth, development, and maturation, by sending out hormones as chemical messengers. Hormones are released into the bloodstream in carefully measured amounts by the endocrine glands, including the pituitary gland, the thyroid, the adrenal gland, the thymus, the pancreas, the ovaries, and the testes. Each type of hormone travels until it reaches a cell with a receptor that it fits as a key fits a lock. This allows the hormone to "turn on" the cell, stimulating it to produce a certain protein or to multiply. When endocrine disruptors enter the body, they mimic hormones and become like a key in a lock, interfering with the normal functions of the endocrine system. Because hormones are effective in tiny quantities, even miniscule quantities of an endocrine-disrupting chemical can cause damage. An endocrine disruptor might block a hormone from doing its job in a receptor, or it might give a signal that is too strong, causing the cell to malfunction. An endocrine disruptor might cause a cell to perform its correct function, but at the wrong time. It also might give a signal that is too weak and also comes at the wrong time.

Because endocrine disruptors eventually make their way into the water system, aquatic animals bear the brunt of the damage. Some of them have been found to have misshapen and undersized sex organs. Male fish and amphibians, for example, may develop smaller testes, suffer from reduced sperm production, develop ovaries and produce eggs, or develop as females. Female organisms may develop male traits, such as penises. After the parents' exposure to endocrine disruptors, the numbers of males and females born may be skewed, with many more males being born than females or more females than males. The offspring may develop poorly or have reproductive-system problems, or the population may be reduced due to limited reproductive success.

Endocrine disruption does not just affect the reproductive system: The seabirds known as cormorants develop cross-bill syndrome, in which their bills are crossed, making them unable to feed. Terns are born with birth defects. Frogs are born with three legs, and fish grow large tumors. Among the many effects seen in humans are reproductive problems such as infertility or spontaneous abortion (miscarriage) and neurological disorders.

Some of the worst POPs have been taken off the market in the developed nations. **DDT** (dichlorodiphenyltrichloroethane), a popular insecticide that was banned in 1973, disrupted the ability of some female birds, including bald eagles and peregrine falcons, to manufacture calcium. As a result, the birds laid eggs with extremely thin shells that broke when the mother sat on them, causing the populations of the susceptible species to plummet. Other pesticides have also been banned. Still, with 660,000 tons (600,000 metric tons) of pesticides (more than one-fifth of the world total) being added to fields in North America each year, an enormous quantity of chemicals is entering the environment. One type, chlorophenoxy herbicides, has been blamed for the 200% higher rate of birth defects in infants in rural, wheat-producing counties of the United States than in rural, non-wheat-producing counties.

In many developing countries, the situation with POPs is even worse. Environmental regulations are not followed, and the use of many chemicals that have been banned in developed countries continues. Also, the farmers spraying these chemicals do not have the money to buy protective suits or may live in climates where it is too hot to wear them, resulting in direct exposure. Eighty percent of deaths from pesticides occur in the developing world. Besides harming farmers and their families, these chemicals become part of the surrounding ecosystem.

Soil Loss

Intensive farming greatly increases the erosion rate of farmland. Plowing loosens the earth, and monoculture farming leaves it exposed for part of the year. Without protection, the ground is vulnerable to rain, wind, and gravity. Loose soil exposed to the elements is easily and rapidly eroded. When erosion is extreme, deep gullies cut into and remove the soil. The gullies increase in size as more soil is lost. Fine soil may be blown away by wind, leaving coarser and less fertile sand behind.

Marginal lands—on hillsides, in tropical rain forests, along the edges of deserts—are especially vulnerable to soil erosion. For example, soils that are exposed on hillsides are easily washed downhill.

In general, most soil that erodes is the nutrient-rich topsoil. Artificial fertilizers must be added to make up for losses of soil nutrients, or the land will not be as productive. The eroded sediments are deposited in places where they are not wanted, such as reservoirs, wildlife habitats, and navigable waterways.

About one-third of the world's farmland is currently eroding at 7 to 100 times the rate that soil is forming. China has the highest rate of soil loss, with a national annual average loss of about 18 tons per acre (40 metric tons per hectare). In some locations, soil is lost at 25 tons per acre (48 metric tons per hectare) per year. If every location lost soil at that rate, the entire world's topsoil would be eroded in 150 years.

Since the arrival of Europeans, the United States has lost about one-third of its topsoil. The rate of soil loss is 8 tons per acre (7.2 metric tons per hectare). The midwestern breadbasket has lost one third of its topsoil in just 100 years, with soil eroding 30 times faster than it is forming. In some states, including Iowa and Missouri, soil is lost at nearly twice the nation's average, an annual rate of 16 tons per acre (35 metric tons per hectare). In the early 1980s, the nation was losing 3 billion tons (2.7 billion metric tons) of topsoil a year, an amount equal to the topsoil on 3 million acres (1.2 million hectares). This amount of soil could produce 7 million tons (6.3 million metric tons) of grain; enough, at average world consumption levels, to feed 21 million people.

Erosion can be prevented by covering the soil to reduce the force of the wind and rain. Soil can be protected by adding mulch (organic material) to hold it in place while plants grow. Strip cropping alternates a row of a crop that leaves the ground exposed with a row of a crop that grows close to the ground so it can catch blowing soil. Trees may be planted around the field to break the force of the wind while the crops are planted in rows perpendicular to the wind's direction. To prevent water erosion, steep hillsides can be terraced, and gentler slopes can be contoured. In the tropics, trees above the fields shelter the crops from the force of the rain and keep direct sunlight from baking the ground and breaking down organic materials.

Erosion rates in the United States have been reduced since 1985, when Congress created the United States Conservation Reserve Program (CRP). The CRP pays farmers to plant highly erodable cropland with grass or trees instead of food crops. Within a few years of its creation, the CRP had removed some 35 million acres (14 million hectares) of cropland, nearly one-tenth of the nation's total, from production.

WRAP-UP

Many experts believe that modern agricultural practices brought about by the Green Revolution have turned an activity that had been sustainable for millennia—family farmers protecting their land and other resources in order to survive—into one that focuses on short-term profits. This focus has required the use of an enormous amount of fossil fuels to grow food: between 1 and 10 calories of fossil fuels (for fertilizers, pesticides, mechanization, and transportation) to create one calorie of plant food. As fossil fuels become scarcer, more expensive, and ultimately depleted, this amount of energy input cannot be maintained. In addition to energy costs, modern agriculture takes an enormous toll on the soil. Most of the best soils are already being cultivated; and as human populations increase, more lands, even if they are not optimal for farming, will be needed for food production.

Meat Production

Grasslands, whether they are natural or converted forests, provide forage for grazing animals that are raised for their meat. This chapter discusses how grazing animals compact the soil and carry seeds into regions where the plants are not native, among other impacts. In arid and semiarid regions, overgrazed lands may turn into desert. In developed nations, much meat is now produced in enormous factory farms, where animals live in very unnatural conditions. Factory farms produce meat cheaply, but they use great amounts of fossil fuels and create an enormous amount of pollution.

RANCHING

Rangeland is open land where domesticated animals roam and graze for their food. The best grazing land is grassland, although forests are sometimes logged to make way for ranching, or the ranching begins after an area has been logged for its trees. This practice has been taking place in tropical wet and dry forests in Central and South America for centuries.

Before the arrival of widespread irrigation, the western United States was too arid for agriculture, so the region was used as rangeland. Cow herders moved cattle from place to place, wherever the grass was good. By the end of the nineteenth century, more lands were privately owned, and barbed-wire fences were put up to divide the open prairies. Railroad companies supported fence construction to keep cattle from wandering onto their tracks. Although the open range is gone, huge ranches still exist. One of the world's largest, the King Ranch in Texas, is 825,000 acres (3,340 sq. km), larger than the state of Rhode Island.

Ranching is a common activity in former tropical rain forest land and is responsible for a great deal of deforestation. In the 1960s and 1970s, the Brazilian government began subsidizing the creation of large cattle ranches, so ranch owners today are wealthy and politically connected. Although the sale of beef does bring in foreign capital that helps the country's economy, cattle ranching is responsible for more than 30% of the Amazon's deforestation. About 70% of the beef is raised for local consumption, and the rest goes to foreign markets.

Even if the land is not altered to accommodate the cattle, the cattle still impact the land. When cattle move from place to place, they carry the seeds of nonnative grasses in their digestive tracts and deposit them in areas where the grasses have never grown before. People also have intentionally introduced nonnative grasses, called **invasive** or **alien species**, to regions to provide forage for the animals. (Invasive or alien species are organisms that have been introduced by human activities into a location where they are not native.) Buffelgrass (*Cenchrus ciliaris* or *Pennisetum ciliare*), a native of Africa, was introduced to the Arizona desert for this reason. The grasses grow well after a rain and provide fuel for fires, which, in turn, help the buffelgrass to sprout, so after each fire there is more of the nonnative grass. This cycle has been a disaster for portions of the Sonoran desert, where cacti and other plants are not adapted to fire. Once the cacti have burned away, the buffelgrass takes over the landscape.

When grasslands are grazed for too long, without allowing sufficient time for plant life to recover, the soil becomes trampled so that the grasses are not able to grow again: The land has been overgrazed. Overgrazing can lead to **desertification**.

DESERTIFICATION

The expansion of deserts into formerly productive lands, either agricultural, ranchland, or forest, is called desertification. This process often takes place at the fringes of a desert in an arid or semiarid environment. Although desertification is sometimes caused by a decrease in rainfall, human activities are more often to blame.

Desertification primarily follows the degradation of the soil by deforestation, overgrazing, and salinization. Deforestation and overgrazing decrease plant cover, which increases erosion and makes the land less hospitable for new plants. In developing countries, the soil nutrients that were taken up by trees or animals are burned as firewood or as animal dung for heat and to cook food. Burning destroys the nutrients and also the chance that the region will recover its fertility. Salinization is caused by excess irrigation, as described in Chapter 5.

A significant example of desertification can be seen in the semiarid Sahal region south of the Sahara Desert of Africa. Traditionally, the Sahal was populated by nomadic tribes, who kept their populations low, migrated frequently by following the rains, and were careful not to overgraze an area. In recent times, the nomadic tribes have been forced to remain in one spot due to the enforcement of national boundaries and the initiation of intensive agriculture. The use of groundwater and the relative abundance of rain in the 1960s allowed the Sahel region's population to grow. This proved disastrous when the worst drought of the century hit from 1968 to 1973. During that time, nearly 250,000 people and 3.5 million cattle died of starvation, and the Sahara expanded southward by about 100 miles (150 km).

Between the western United States, sub-Saharan Africa, the Middle East, western Asia, parts of Central and South America, and Australia, more than 100,000 square miles (350,000 sq. km) of land are lost to

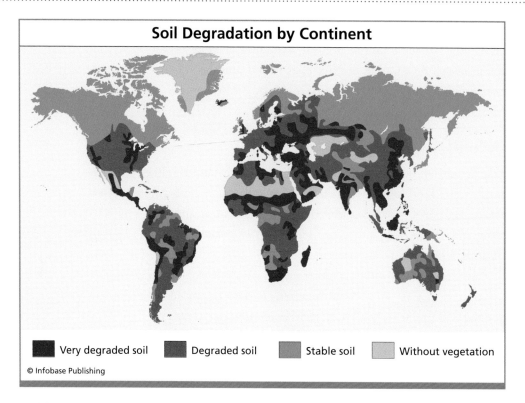

Soil Degradation by Continent

Very degraded soil   Degraded soil   Stable soil   Without vegetation

© Infobase Publishing

Soil degradation occurs all over the world for a variety of reasons, including deforestation, overgrazing, and desertification. The end result is soil exhausted of value for agricultural use, which negatively impacts economies around the globe.

desertification each year. A 2004 United Nations report warns that one-third of the world's land surface is at risk for desertification and that one-fifth of the world's population is threatened by the potential impacts of this land change.

FACTORY FARMS

Although the image of cows grazing over enormous expanses of grassland is still dear to people, most farm animals in developed countries barely see the light of day. Fully 78% of the beef produced in the United States comes from feedlots, where cattle live shoulder to shoulder and are fed corn and wheat, a diet that is not natural to grazers.

These confined animal feeding operations (CAFO), or factory farms, are enormous production facilities that, in some cases, may house up to hundreds of thousands of animals, including pigs, cattle, dairy cows, and chickens. On a typical North Carolina hog farm, for example, between 880 and 1,220 animals live together in a barn with slatted floors for the waste to pass through. Most of the state's 10 million hogs being grown for slaughter live in this manner.

CAFOs are designed to grow animals for slaughter or to produce milk or eggs as quickly and cheaply as possible. These farms rely heavily on mechanization. In a factory poultry farm, machines deliver feed and water and remove wastes automatically. When a chicken reaches the desired weight, it is processed in an assembly line. This efficiency has decreased the price of chicken so that what was once a luxury is now a staple item in many people's diets. This cheap meat comes at a price: it takes 35 calories of fossil fuel (for fertilizers and pesticides for feed, mechanization, and transportation) to make one calorie of beef, and 68 calories of fossil fuel to create one calorie of pork.

Because the capital outlay to start a mechanized farm is high, factory farms are often owned by large corporations. Farmers are contracted to grow the animals for these corporations. The corporations take the product but leave behind the pollutants. One reason that CAFOs are major polluters is the sheer numbers of animals they process. For example, feedlots in the United States produce nearly 300 billion pounds (136 million metric tons) of manure daily. Because the feedlots are usually located far from farmer's fields, the manure, which is rich in phosphates and nitrates, is usually not used as fertilizer but is kept in waste ponds, where it releases the greenhouse gas methane. Some operations use the manure as fertilizer, but often too much is put on the fields for the crops to absorb: The excess nutrients run off into the water supply and cause eutrophication.

The runoff from CAFOs also includes whatever chemicals or pharmaceuticals were used to facilitate raising the animals. Because they are packed so close together, the animals can easily become sick, and antibiotics are given to prevent the spread of disease. However, excess use of antibiotics poses a threat to animals and humans as bacteria develop resistance to the antibiotics. Chemical pollutants and pharmaceuticals may also harm fish and other aquatic life and contaminate drinking water supplies. Factory farms are not yet as widespread in the developing world as are family farms.

WRAP-UP

Meat production is inefficient because only about 10% of the calories an animal takes in are available in its flesh for food. (The animals burn the rest of the calories for warmth, for movement, and for reproduction.) On ranches, grazing animals convert grass, which is not digestible by humans, into useful food, but the health of the land may be compromised by overgrazing. In factory farms, the animals' lives are so restricted that many more of the calories they eat are converted to food calories, but at enormous costs in fossil fuels and pollution. Although CAFOs do not bear much resemblance to family farms, such large-scale feeding operations operate under laws that were designed to protect small farms that did not house enough animals to cause major environmental damage. Because of this, the current rules are insufficient to deal with the problems caused by large meat-production facilities.

Sustainable Agriculture

This chapter discusses how, in the past few decades, a backlash has taken place against industrialized agriculture, and a movement has grown to make farming more environmentally sound. Sustainable agriculture strives to promote environmental stewardship and stable, prosperous farm communities by making small individual farms profitable.

SUSTAINABLE FARMING PRACTICES

Growers who farm sustainably apply the principles of natural ecosystems to agricultural landscapes. To avoid the risks of agricultural monocultures, which are vulnerable to pests and disease and deplete the soil of nutrients, farmers plant a diverse assortment of crops that grow in different seasons. Crop rotation also counteracts the problems of monocultures; although farmers may grow only one type of crop at a time, they plant different crops in different years. Each of these strategies decreases nutrient loss from the soil and keeps the plants from competing for resources. Some crops, such as legumes, even replenish some nutrients. Farmers who adhere to sustainable agriculture practices do not utilize genetically modified organisms, artificial fertilizers, pesticides, or other synthetic chemicals. They also avoid the use of nonrenewable resources such as fossil fuels for farming or for transporting goods.

Sustainable farming also follows the principles of **organic farming**. A product labeled organic must meet standards set by the federal government. This means that crops and animals are not exposed to synthetic chemicals or pharmaceuticals. Organic farming takes a more flexible approach to dealing with unwanted insects and weeds than conventional farming. Organic farmers tolerate some loss of crops to pests. They also carefully select crops to minimize the chance that they will be harmed by insects. Using integrated pest management, growers design a plan to attract species that will eat the pests. For example, a crop that attracts beneficial insects might be planted in between rows of a crop that attracts pests that the beneficial insects will eat.

In sustainable agriculture, only fertilizers from natural sources such as manure, rock phosphate, and recycled crop waste are used. Often these nutrients are produced elsewhere on the farm. To protect the land's natural organic matter and nutrients, the soil is treated carefully to avoid erosion and degradation. Although they may irrigate, growers try not to use more water than can be replenished naturally.

Animals grown sustainably are fed only organic feed, are allowed outdoors, and are not raised in crowded conditions. Use of pharmaceuticals such as antibiotics is not allowed. Horses and cows work on the farm and provide manure.

Sustainable farming is best done in communities where farmers can share machinery, manure, and expertise. Their food is sold locally through specialty shops or at farmers' markets where they sell products directly to consumers. One recent and growing phenomenon is Community Supported Agriculture (CSA). A CSA is a group made up of growers and consumers. Consumers buy a membership in a CSA in advance of the growing season, usually at a cost of about $20 or $25 for each week goods will be delivered to them. Having the capital up front gives the farmers money to grow the crops and also spreads the financial risk associated with sustainable farming. No matter how bad the weather is, or how much produce is consumed by insect pests, each farmer receives the same amount of money from the CSA members.

 ## Theresa Mauer: *Applying Ecological Principles to Agricultural Practices*

Teresa Maurer has found the perfect way to meld her interests in biology and in growing, cooking, and eating food that is healthy and good for the environment. Using her biology background, Maurer helps farmers understand and use sustainable agriculture practices.

Maurer began her career investigating the ecology of insect-plant relationships in the grasslands of Eastern Oregon. Her field site was located on a nature preserve in the middle of a working ranch. The rancher told the scientist about cattle grazing and grassland management while she shared with him what she learned about the plant and insect species she was studying. A few years later, at a presentation on using principles of grasslands ecology to design ways to produce food and fiber that are less harmful to soil, water, air, and people, Maurer saw the way to combine her interests in biology and food production. Since that time, Maurer has used ecological principles to design better agricultural practices and has helped farmers convert to using these sustainable practices.

In her position with the National Center for Appropriate Technology (NCAT), Maurer oversees the sustainable agriculture information service, which provides answers to farmers' questions via the telephone, the Internet, and in nationwide workshops. She and her staff help farmers convert to organic farming by advising them on how to meet the complex organic standards. They encourage using sheep and goats, instead of herbicides, for vegetation management. Maurer's group also links local farmers with local chefs, giving the farmers a market for their products and letting the chefs know what is seasonally available in their region.

During the past 25 years, Maurer has seen consumers develop a greater awareness of how and where their food is produced and has seen the number of groups working in sustainable and organic agriculture grow from about 30 to more than 500. She says that, while at the federal level there is more recognition of sustainable practices, promoting them is still a tiny portion of the federal agriculture budget.

If the bounty is good, the members benefit; and if the bounty is bad, the farmers still stay in business. The farmers can sell extra produce at farmers' markets, as well. CSAs provide a way for small farmers to compete against large agribusiness corporations that have enormous resources to help them weather the bad times.

The basis of organic farming is small-scale, local operations. Not long ago, a product labeled organic was also likely to have been raised sustainably. However, the organic foods market is growing at 20% a year, which has brought about the growth of large, industrial organic farms. Although the plants and animals are raised according to federal standards for organic food, the effort is not necessarily made to grow the food in a sustainable manner. Though they are fed organic grain, the animals are still packed together in large barns, and abundant fossil fuels are used both for mechanized farming and to transport goods all over the world. It is these large agribusinesses that supply the large market chains with organic produce and meats.

One of the tenets of sustainable farming is that the food should be priced responsibly. If growing crops without using artificial fertilizers, pesticides, and fossil fuels costs more, then the food should cost more. Food produced by big agribusiness is not priced responsibly: Many of its costs are not paid by either the growers or the consumers. For example, the cost of the excess nutrients used on crops is borne by the fishers who can no longer harvest in the eutrophic lakes or marine dead zones created by the runoff of those nutrients. The price of fossil-fuel use is **air pollution** and acid rain, a price that is paid by those who breathe the air or rely on resources in the aquatic ecosystems and forests that suffer the damage brought by the pollution's downwind effects.

However, large supermarket chains are often most concerned about short-term profits, a concern that leads to products being priced irresponsibly. For example, if it is cheaper to raise grass-fed beef in New Zealand and then fly it to the United States, despite the enormous amount of pollution and greenhouse gases this generates, that is the grass-fed beef the large supermarkets will sell. Small farmers who raise their products sustainably are concerned that allowing agribusiness to label products organic that are not also sustainable dilutes the high standards to which small organic farms would like the label to be held.

As Michael Pollan—a journalism professor at the University of California, Berkeley—said of large agribusiness going organic, in his May 2006 *New York Times* blog, "The result is a greener factory farm, to be sure, but a factory nevertheless."

It is unclear whether sustainable, organic farming can completely replace conventional farming. In a 22-year study of crop yield, researchers at Cornell University discovered that organically farmed soybeans and corn had the same yield as crops farmed by conventional methods. As a bonus, it took less energy to grow the organic crops, and they had no pesticide residues. A survey of farms in the United States concluded that organic crops yielded between 95% and 100% as much as conventional crops. Yet a 21-year Swiss study found the yield for organic crops to be only 80% as high as for conventional crops. On the positive side, the Swiss study found that much less money was spent on fertilizers and energy. Other studies have shown that small farms produce more food than large farms, and **polycultures** (where multiple species are grown together) are more productive than monocultures.

WRAP-UP

It is not enough to seek out foods with an organic label. Eating responsibly requires finding food that is grown locally, organically, and sustainably. Sustainable agriculture is growing as consumers seek to have more of a connection with the food they eat and with the environment it comes from. Organizations such as CSAs make it easier for people to connect with farmers and the land. Yet, despite the growth of sustainable and organic farms, the much larger surge in recent decades has occurred in the opposite direction. However, food consumption is one area in which people collectively can make a big difference in how land is used and how agriculture is practiced. As Pollan suggests, "Vote with your fork."

PART THREE

MINERAL RESOURCE EXTRACTION

Mining

Mineral resources are essential for modern society. Useful minerals can be categorized as gems, metals, or nonmetals. This chapter describes how geologists seek mineral deposits in geologic settings where ores are likely to form. When they find a deposit, the scientists work to determine its size and the quality of its mineral content. Economic factors help to decide whether the deposit is worth mining. If the answer is yes, the valuable rock is extracted from the ground surface or below ground. Many types of mining require the movement of tremendous amounts of rock material, and extracting the useful minerals from the rock may involve the addition of heat or chemicals.

MINERAL RESOURCES

Humans have shown great ingenuity in how they use the Earth's minerals resources. At the beginning of civilization, stone was fashioned into arrowheads, knives, axes, and other tools, all of which helped Stone

Age humans exploit an array of geological and biological resources. Since those days, people have learned to use a wider variety of geologic materials: They have molded precious metals into jewelry, and fertilized crops with phosphates. They have used copper wires to facilitate communication, silicon chips to process information, and petroleum to fuel travel.

Mining is the process used to extract useful minerals and rocks found at or near the Earth's surface. **Gemstones**—such as diamond, ruby, emerald, garnet, and topaz—are prized for their beauty. A few of them are used for industry. For example, diamond, an extremely hard mineral, is used for the precision cutting of other materials. Metals—shiny elements that can conduct heat and electricity—include copper, tin, iron, lead, gold, silver, platinum, and mercury. Some metals, such as gold and silver, are prized for their beauty, while others are valued for their physical properties. Nonmetals are also useful: granite as a building stone, calcite as a raw material for cement, and gypsum for plaster and sheet rock, for example.

Although valuable minerals are scattered throughout the Earth's crust and waters, most minerals can be mined only where they have been concentrated by Earth processes. In some rare deposits, the elements are pure—such as the native (pure) gold that can be found in veins—but in most deposits the desired elements are contained in molecules that make up minerals. Rock that contains sufficient amounts of one or more valuable minerals for profitable mining is called **ore**. Note, then, that the definition of ore is economic, rather than geologic.

An ore's grade refers to the level of its concentration in the rock. High-grade ore is more desirable because it is highly concentrated and easier to refine than low-grade ore. However, as high-grade ores are mined out, mining lower-grade deposits becomes economically feasible. The environmental costs of mining lower-grade ores are usually higher because a large amount of rock must be processed to extract the valuable material. The rock that is discarded after the ore is mined is considered waste.

About 40 metals are commercially valuable, but most of today's mining operations concentrate on only three—aluminum, iron, and copper.

(Other important metals include lead, silver, gold, vanadium, titanium, and tellurium. Important nonmetals are salt, gypsum, and phosphates.)

HOW ORES FORM

Mining geologists look for places where Earth processes have concentrated valuable materials into ore. The main processes that concentrate ores are described below.

Magmatic Processes

Metals that are present in magma form distinctive minerals that crystallize as the magma cools. Metallic minerals are heavy and sink to the floor of the magma chamber as a pluton forms. If this pluton is later pushed up to the Earth's surface, the metallic minerals may be minable. Diamonds form at high pressures deep in the Earth's crust and are torpedoed to the surface within magma pipes. Volcanic gases are laden with sulfur that can also be mined.

Hydrothermal Processes

Hydrothermal (hot water) processes produce more types of deposits and larger quantities of ore than all other ore-forming processes combined. The hot fluids come off a cooling magma, or they may originate as groundwater traveling near a magma body or seawater flowing into a deep sea volcano. The hot water dissolves metals from the rock or magma, transports them through pores or cracks in rock, and finally deposits them in concentrated ore bodies.

There are many types of hydrothermal deposits. Metals that precipitate from fluids in fractures in a rock create vein deposits. Metal-rich fluids can also soak a permeable rock, leaving behind a large but less concentrated ore body called a **disseminated ore** deposit. The valuable material in these deposits may be so dispersed that ore concentrations may be less than one ounce (28 grams) per ton. Porphyry copper deposits are disseminated ores that are rich in copper, molybdenum, gold, silver, and in other metals. Many metals are present in porphyry copper and in other ore deposits as sulfide minerals.

Sulfides are made from one or more sulfur ions combined with one or more metal ions. Common sulfide ore minerals include the iron sulfide pyrite (commonly called *fool's gold*) and chalcopyrite, a copper iron sulfide that accounts for about half of all copper ore mined today. Hydrothermal processes may also produce ores of iron, zinc, lead, tin, and tungsten.

Metamorphic Processes

Metamorphism produces several types of ore deposits. Marble, a popular building stone, is metamorphosed limestone. Many gemstones, such as garnet, are metamorphic minerals. Other useful metamorphic minerals are graphite (the "lead" part of a pencil) and asbestos, which has a number of important industrial uses.

Sedimentary Processes

Coal is a sedimentary rock formed of ancient land plants. In warm, wet swamps, the dead bodies of fast-growing plants accumulate so rapidly that little oxygen can get to them. Because few bacteria live in this oxygen-free environment, the plants do not decay effectively and convert to peat. As peat sinks deeper into the ground, it is compressed and transformed into coal. The more heat and pressure the coal experiences, the higher quality coal it will become.

Two sedimentary processes—sorting and evaporation—create ore deposits. **Placer** deposits are formed when valuable ores, most commonly gold, are weathered out of the rock they are in and then carried away by a stream. Because the ore minerals are heavy, when the stream slows down, the dense, heavy particles fall to the bottom and are concentrated. Gold placers were very important to the development of the western United States. The forty-niners of the California Gold Rush mined for placer gold in the streams of the Sierra Nevada mountains. In the beginning of the Gold Rush, some miners struck it rich simply by swirling rock and water around in giant pans and retrieving the gold that had settled to the bottom.

Minerals such as halite, gypsum, carbonates, and potassium salts precipitate out of a solution as the water evaporates. Iron comes from banded iron formations, which are very rich bodies of iron ore that formed primarily between 2.6 and 1.9 billion years ago, when plant life first became abundant. First, the plants produced oxygen as a byproduct of photosynthesis. Then the oxygen combined with iron that was free-floating in the ocean; and, finally, the iron oxides precipitated from the water. It is no accident that the giant American auto manufacturers located their plants near Lake Superior, where ancient banded iron formations are common.

Weathering Processes

Weathering processes form ores by creating new minerals. For example, clay minerals—used for porcelain or for lining landfills and ditches—are formed from the weathering of feldspar minerals. Weathering processes also form ores by concentrating valuable minerals. In warm, tropical, or subtropical regions, rainwater percolates through the soil, picking up soluble ions but leaving behind insoluble ones. This process concentrates these ions to form bauxite ore, which may consist of nearly 65% aluminum.

Weathering can also increase the concentration of ore minerals around ore bodies. Rainwater collects metal ions as it travels through a diffuse ore deposit and then reprecipitates them in nearby soils. This process may concentrate tens to hundreds of times more ore than was found in the original ore body. Because these enriched zones are so economically valuable, most of them have already been mined out.

Stone, Gravel, and Sand

Because of their strength and beauty, some rocks are valued as building stones and are found on facades, floors, countertops, and as tombstones. Common building stones come from each of the three major rock types. Granite, marble, slate, limestone, and sandstone are among the most popular. Sand and gravel are used for building roads and stabilizing beaches. These materials are mined from deposits left by streams, glaciers, wind, and ocean waves. Each year, more money is made from the mining of sand and gravel than from the mining of gold.

Phosphates

Phosphate fertilizers replenish soil with lost nutrients or make soils that are nutrient deficient suitable for farming. Phosphorus is a major constituent of the mineral apatite, which is found in bones, teeth, and shells. Most economically viable deposits of apatite are the result of the collection of plankton shells in productive regions of the ocean. These apatite-rich sediments are often found at continental margins. Some of them have been moved onto continental regions by Earth processes. The largest phosphate deposits in the United States are found

Ore Types and Their Uses

COMMODITY	USES
Aluminum	engineering, transportation, aerospace
Coal	energy
Copper	wire, pipes, electrical uses, home products
Diamonds	jewelry, industry
Gold	jewelry, dentistry, electronics, ornamentation
Halite (salt)	food preservation and flavor
Iron	structures, steel
Lead	batteries, bullets, radiation shields
Limestone	building stone, neutralizing acids
Nickel	industry, home products
Phosphate	fertilizer, water softener in detergents
Platinum	jewelry, industry, medications
Tin	corrosion resistance, food preservation, electrical uses, chemical uses
Uranium	shielding, nuclear power

in sedimentary rocks in Florida. Phosphates are also mined from sea-bird guano on islands that serve as seabird rookeries.

ORE DEPOSITS

To determine whether a mineral deposit is worth mining, geologists must calculate how much it will cost to mine the ore body and how much money will be generated by mining it. The decision whether or not to mine can change instantly if the price of the ore goes up or down drastically, if a new technology lowers the cost of mining, if an important source of the ore becomes depleted, or if a new source is discovered. Some ores and their uses are shown in the table on page 82.

MINING TECHNIQUES

Which technique is used to mine an ore depends on the type of ore, the type of rock it is located in, and whether it is located at or beneath the ground surface. The two basic types of mining are surface mining and underground mining.

Because surface mining is relatively inexpensive, surface and near-surface deposits are more economic to mine and account for more than two-thirds of the world's annual mineral production. Heavy equipment removes the rock and soil that overlies the ore deposit—the overburden—and then extracts the rock that contains the ore. The five types of surface mining are:

- Strip mining: All of the material overlying the ore body is removed and dumped as waste. On flat terrain, strip mining disturbs large areas. On hillsides, terraces are created to allow access to the ore. Strip mining is commonly used for mining coal seams and tar sands.
- Open pit mining: Similar to strip mining, except that the overburden is removed to create an open pit, which is enlarged until the ore deposit is completely removed. Gold, copper, and other metals are taken from open pit mines.

Giant excavators work in the Garzwieler II, a coal mine in western Germany, with the coal-fired power plant visible in the background. *(Achim Holzem / iStockphoto)*

Pits may be thousands of feet deep and more than a mile (1.6 km) across.

⊕ Mountaintop removal: If a deposit is as much as 1,000 feet (300 m) beneath a hill, forests will be clear cut, and the top of the hill removed by explosives to expose the mineral deposit. This technique is commonly used to mine coal.

⊕ Dredging: Dredging is used for underwater mineral deposits. A specially designed bucket is deployed behind a ship on a chain and dragged along the bottom to collect the valuable minerals that are lying on the seafloor. The difficulty and expense of this method has hindered the development of deep sea mining operations.

⊕ Placer mining: Placers, or alluvial deposits, were panned early in the California Gold Rush. As the gold became scarcer, hydraulic mining, a more powerful method of excavation,

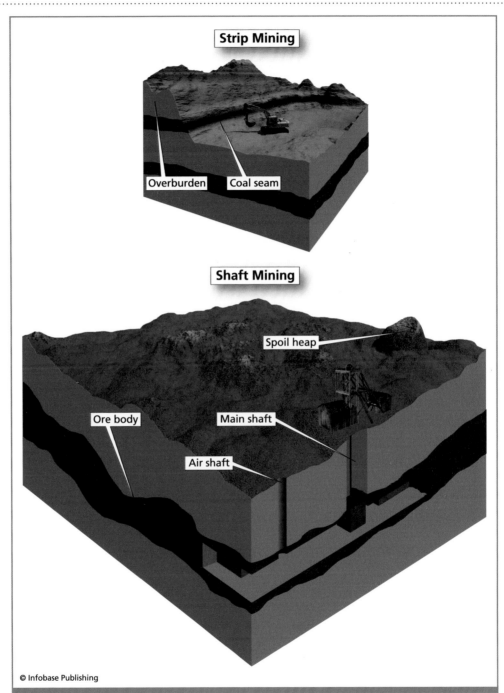

Strip Mining

Overburden   Coal seam

Shaft Mining

Spoil heap

Ore body   Main shaft

Air shaft

© Infobase Publishing

Minerals can be removed from the Earth via strip mining (top) and shaft mining (bottom), among other techniques.

took over. In hydraulic mining, a strong jet of water breaks heavy minerals away from sediments. The sediments are then run through a rippled wooden trough known as a sluice box. Because gold is heavier than the other materials, it drops into the ripples while the other materials are washed away.

Underground mining requires miners to blast and then tunnel into overlying rock to gain access to ores that lie farther below the surface. Underground mining is done only when surface methods would be too costly or unsafe. The type of underground method chosen depends on the size, shape, and orientation of the ore body; the depth of the ore body; the grade of the ore; and the strength of the surrounding rock. A mine shaft is built to provide miners access to the ore. The shaft can cut horizontally, vertically, or diagonally into the hillside, depending on how the ore body is oriented.

ORE EXTRACTION

Once the ore-bearing rock has been collected, it is crushed to a size suitable for easy extraction. Many processes are available for extracting the valuable minerals from the waste rock. The process that is chosen depends on the type of ore, the minerals it is bound up with, and its grade. Extraction processes may be used in combination until the desired mineral is nearly pure. A few of the processes for extracting ore are as follows:

⊕ **Heap leaching**: Ore is crushed to an appropriate size and placed in enormous heaps that can be hundreds of yards long and up to 30 yards (27 m) high. A dilute chemical solution is then sprayed on the heap; for example, sulfuric acid is used for copper oxide ores, while sodium cyanide is used for gold ores.

⊕ Froth flotation: A compound (often pine oil) is added to the ground ore, which is then placed in a water bath. Air is pumped through the bath. The added compound, along with the valuable mineral, attaches to the air bubbles. The ore floats at the top of the bath and can be skimmed off the surface.

⊕ **Smelting**: In this process, rock is roasted in a furnace with the appropriate compounds, which causes the material to segregate into layers. Smelting encourages chemical reactions that cause the metal to be released.

⊕ Chemical reduction: A chemical reducing agent (which adds electrons), such as carbon (coke), is mixed with the ore and heated. The oxygen from the ore moves into the carbon to produce carbon dioxide and carbon monoxide. The metal is then left in a reduced state, and a fluxing agent, such as limestone, removes the accompanying waste rock.

⊕ Sulfide extraction: To extract metal from sulfide, the rock is heated until two liquids form. One is waste; the other contains metal sulfide and some impurities.

⊕ **Electrowinning:** The ore is put into solution, and an electrical charge drives the metal ions onto a foil cathode (a **cathode** is the positively charged terminal of a battery or voltaic cell) made of the same metal. After electrowinning, the cathode and metal can be sold or molded into a different form.

Copper, one of the three most-mined mineral commodities, provides a good example of how ore is extracted from rock. Copper ore is most commonly found bound up in copper sulfide and copper oxide minerals in porphyry copper deposits. The ore, which usually contains less than 1% copper, is dug or blasted from an open pit or an underground mine. It is then crushed into walnut-sized pieces and ground to a powder.

The copper-bearing minerals are concentrated by froth flotation. After the copper froth is skimmed from the mixture and dried, one of two methods is used to refine the concentrated copper, as follows:

⊕ Oxide ores are heap leached with weak sulfuric acid to produce a weak copper sulfate solution, which is further refined by electrowinning. Precious metals may also be extracted from the solution.

⊕ Sulfide ores undergo smelting, which causes the iron-copper material to sink. The iron-copper metal is mixed with air, lime, silica, and sometimes scrap copper, which attracts the copper ions in the solution. The solution then undergoes electrowinning.

Once the copper is nearly pure, it is made into wires, logs, slabs, and bricks. Used copper is also recycled, a process that begins with smelting.

WRAP-UP

Earth processes concentrate minerals to form ore deposits. Whether a mineral deposit will be mined is an economic decision based on the amount of money it will cost to remove the rock from the ground, extract the ore from the rock, and transport the ore to where it will be used. A mineral deposit that is regarded as valuable one day may not be valuable the next if the price of the commodity drops or the cost of extracting it goes up. How ores are mined and extracted depends on the ore type and where it is located.

Environmental Effects of Mining

Mining takes a tremendous toll on the environment by generating enormous amounts of waste and pollutants. Gold mining is especially damaging in developed nations, where only very low-grade deposits remain, and in developing nations, where environmental oversight is often weak. According to the Environmental Protection Agency (EPA), hard rock mining is the most polluting industry in the United States. This chapter explores these problems.

POLLUTION FROM MINES

Surface mining clears the landscape, destroying organisms and ecosystems. Disturbed rock and soil erode more easily. Eroded sediments can flow into streams, lakes, and seas and damage aquatic ecosystems. Water and sediments from a mine site are often contaminated with pollutants, particularly **heavy metals** such as lead and mercury, which actually are of heavy weight, or cyanide (from gold mines). This increases the sediments' toxicity.

Smelting requires that the mined ore be heated, which ordinarily requires the burning of great amounts of fossil fuels. Heated ore releases particles (including metal oxides), oils, and other pollutants. In modern mining operations, emission control devices capture these materials; some of these emissions are even mined for metals and other valuable materials. For example, sulfur dioxide can be captured and converted to sulfuric acid that can be used in heap leaching. In countries where mining is not so heavily regulated, enormous amounts of air pollutants, including toxic heavy metals, may be emitted into the atmosphere.

The mining process also creates acid pollutants. Water that comes into contact with rock becomes slightly acidic. Rock that has been disturbed and exposed by mining has a greater surface area for water to access, causing the water to become even more acidic. The acidity can rise to alarming levels if the disturbed rock is made up of sulfides, which are broken down by colonies of bacteria into metal ions and sulfuric acid. The flow of acids from a mine site is called **acid mine drainage**. While a mine remains open, the miners put lime on the rock to keep acid from forming; but once the mine is closed, the practice is abandoned, and acid mine drainage usually begins. The flow of acids through mine waste releases heavy metals such as cadmium, lead, arsenic, manganese, nickel, and copper from the rock, making the solutions that emanate from these mines even more toxic.

The process that forms acid mine drainage also generates heat. Abandoned mine sites may be extremely hot (up to 120°F [50°C]). The pH of these systems may be as low as 0, and some even dip to negative numbers. This high acidity occurs when water evaporates from an acidic pool, leaving behind the hydrogen ions. If an acid mine system has a pH near 3, the iron ions form iron hydroxide. Known as "yellow boy," this yellow-orange compound discolors water and disrupts stream ecosystems. Yellow boy formation produces hydrogen ions, further increasing the system's acidity.

Wetlands are naturally good at cleaning up the pollution from mines. Bacteria change sulfur into a form that can create a chemical bond with heavy metals, causing metal sulfides to precipitate out of the solution. Bacteria and wetland plants also decrease the water's acidity.

In many instances, constructed wetlands are a more cost-effective treatment for mine pollution than artificial treatment plants. Once a wetland is constructed, it can be largely left alone, although mine effluent from it may need additional treatment. On the other hand, a treatment plant must be constructed and maintained and needs money to keep operating. Depending on wetlands to clean up mining pollution takes a long time, however, and is not effective in an environment that is too polluted to support a wetland system.

GOLD MINING

Modern gold mining is arguably the most environmentally destructive form of mining. It is also unique because gold has limited practical use for society. Gold has applications in the electronics and medical equipment industries and is used to back up currency. For example, the United States keeps $122 billion in gold bullion to ensure the value of the country's money (although these days, no country backs up its currency with an equivalent amount of gold). Approximately 80% of gold is used for jewelry. Gold mining is a big business, and about 2,500 tons (80 million troy ounces, or 2.5 billion grams) of gold is mined each year. The growing economies of India and China have joined the developed nations in their hunger for gold. Many of the social and environmental impacts of gold mining are discussed below.

Waste Rock

Gold ore is usually found in rock in native form; thus, gold can be mined at lower concentrations than any other metal. The disseminated gold deposits that are currently being mined typically have about one-quarter ounce per ton (about 7 grams per metric ton) of gold. Hundreds of tons of rock need to be mined to produce one pound (one-half kg) of gold. In some parts of Nevada, about 100 tons (90 metric tons) of earth is moved to find a single ounce, or about one ring's worth (28 grams). (Nevada is the third largest gold producer in the world, after South Africa and Australia, and is responsible for four-fifths of the gold produced in the United States.)

Cyanide

If the metal is present as native gold, the ore is mined, crushed, and placed into heaps. If the gold is bound into a mineral, the rock must first be roasted, chemically altered, or ground until it is ultrafine. Depending on the type of rock and the form of the gold, the preferred method for extracting gold from the rock is heap leaching, using a dilute (about 0.035%) sodium cyanide solution. As the solution trickles through the rock, the cyanide anions dissolve and mix with the gold cations to form the very stable compound sodium cyanoaurite, which then enters into solution. The solution flows out the base of the heap and is next run through activated carbon. The sodium cyanoaurite adsorbs onto the carbon, and the mixture is separated by a screen. A hot, strong solution of sodium cyanide and sodium hydroxide is then used to leach the gold from the carbon. The gold is electrically or chemically removed from this new solution. This process produces enormous amounts of toxic waste, from the cyanide chemical solutions to the cyanide-laced waste rock.

Cyanide is a notorious poison: A teaspoonful (4.8 g) of 2% cyanide solution will kill a human adult. Cyanide blocks the absorption of oxygen by cells and damages the central nervous system, respiratory system, and cardiovascular system. Low doses of cyanide are known to harm mammals, birds, and—in extremely low doses—fish, in which it inhibits the ability to reproduce. At higher doses, cyanide affects the animals' physiology. Cyanide does not bioaccumulate. Therefore, subtoxic exposure over long periods does not seem to cause health problems, nor is it harmful to eat fish containing cyanide at low concentrations. However, cyanide solutions not only collect gold, but also pick up heavy metals such as mercury and arsenic, which are also toxic.

Solar radiation breaks down cyanide, but this process cannot occur underground or in cloudy or rainy conditions. If the cyanide solution becomes acidic, as it will if there is also acid mine drainage, the cyanide turns into an extremely toxic gas. (Cyanide gas was used in the gas chambers of Nazi Germany during the Holocaust.) If the cyanide solution is alkaline, the cyanide will not break down. Even if cyanide does break down, it may decompose into other compounds that are toxic to aquatic organisms, such as cyanate and ammonia. Some of cyanide's breakdown products, such as thiocyanate, bioaccumulate and over time may cause more harm than the cyanide itself. At some mines, the cyanide solutions that are released after the gold has been extracted are captured and recycled.

Following heap leaching, giant quantities of waste rock remain that are badly contaminated with cyanide. This rock is placed in pits that are coated with clay and plastic liners designed to keep the cyanide poison from leaching into the soil and water. The pile is then covered to keep out birds and other animals. Of course, liners sometimes leak, and pits may overflow, which is especially likely to happen after the mine has been abandoned. In 1992, a cyanide spill killed over 11,000 fish along a 50-mile (80 km) stretch of the Lynches River in South Carolina. That same year, a cyanide spill killed all the life along 17 miles (27 km) of the Alamosa River in the San Juan Mountains of southwestern Colorado. The total cleanup costs for the latter spill were more than $150 million.

The worst cyanide spill so far took place at a gold mine in Romania in 2000. Water exposed to cyanide-treated waste rock broke through its containment pond and entered a tributary of the Danube River. Nearly all of the fish in the affected waters were killed, a total of more than 1,000 tons (900 metric tons). The cyanide plume flowed 1,600 miles (2,600 km) down the Danube to the Black Sea. The region's drinking water is likely to be affected for decades.

Water

Gold mining uses tremendous quantities of water, which is costly both environmentally and socially. Besides being the state with the most gold in the United States, Nevada is also the driest and the fastest growing. The state's largest city, Las Vegas, receives only 4.5 inches (11.4 cm) of rain a year. Therefore, it needs to draw water from all around the region. To support its exploding population, the city is look-ing at using groundwater sources in the northern part of the state, the same area where most of the gold mines are located.

Water is involved in gold mining in two ways. Water is used to dilute cyanide for heap leaching, a process that requires an enormous amount of water. Even more significant is the fact that several of Nevada's open pit mines lie beneath aquifers. In these locations, water runs out of the aquifer and into the open pit mine. This wastes enormous amounts of water, which must then be pumped away. The pit at the Goldstrike Mine north of Carlin, Nevada, is 1,600 feet (490 m) below the aquifer. As a result, nearly 10 million gallons (38 million liters) of water are pumped from the aquifer each day to keep the pit dry. Some of that water is used for cyanide leaching, and some goes to nearby communities for irrigation. But much of the water evaporates or flows into the Humboldt River, which has experienced a tremendous increase in flow as a result. Of course, this water is lost as a groundwater resource.

Estimates are that most of the state's mines will be operational for about another decade. Once the mines are abandoned, the pumping will stop, and the pits will fill with water. Most of these man-made lakes will be laden with acids and toxic heavy metals. As the aquifer empties into the pits, it will suck water out of the Humboldt River so that the water levels in the river will become unnaturally low.

Mercury

Gold mining adds mercury pollutants to the air and water. Gold smelters contribute more than 3% of airborne mercury pollution in the United States, the same as is produced by about 25 coal-fired power plants. Some of this airborne mercury appears to be making its way into Nevada's northern neighbor, Idaho, where one reservoir has mercury levels 10 times higher than have ever been measured in the state. Mercury also enters the environment from the gold mines' waste rocks.

Mercury is probably the most damaging of heavy metals. Once released into the air, it cools and turns into aerosol droplets, which may travel hundreds of miles (km) through the atmosphere and eventually rain to the ground or into the water to find its way into sediment. Bacteria then convert this mercury into organic mercury, usually **methyl**

mercury. This dangerous compound is easily absorbed through the skin, lungs, and guts of animals. Methyl mercury is extremely toxic and is poisonous to some algae and to the larvae of some small invertebrates (animals without backbones). This compound bioaccumulates in top predators, including fish eaten by people, such as tuna. Humans are very sensitive to methyl mercury: It causes brain, liver, and kidney damage.

GOLD MINING IN THE DEVELOPING WORLD

In the developed nations, the richest gold deposits have already been or are currently being depleted. To satisfy the world's growing demand, about 70% of gold is now being mined in developing countries. Entities such as the World Bank, in an effort to alleviate world poverty, facilitate gold mining in developing nations in the hope that the multinational corporations involved in mining will bring investment, infrastructure, and jobs to these poor areas. To some extent this is true.

Yet, there is another side to this issue. In most developing nations, environmental regulations and enforcement are weak. Mining companies take advantage of this by engaging in practices that would not be tolerated in the wealthier nations. Some of the problems have arisen due to these conditions are as follows:

- In 1995, a nearly 800,000-gallon (3-million l) spill of cyanide flowed into a tributary of the Essequibo River, which is the main water source for the country of Guyana.
- A lawsuit was brought by a province in the Philippines against a Canadian gold company, alleging that its wastes ruined a river, a bay, and a coral reef.
- The world's largest mining company closed a mine in Papua New Guinea after it destroyed more than 2,400 acres (9.7 square km) of rain forest. The Australian company decided that the mine was too environmentally destructive, although the mine is now being operated by another company.

- The Grasberg mine in Indonesia, operated by an American gold company, will create 6 billion tons (5.4 billion metric tons) of waste over its life, twice the amount of material that was excavated to create the Panama Canal. The waste is being dumped in the mountains and down a river, where it poisons the aquatic ecosystem and its wetlands and has now reached the ocean. Acid mine drainage now trickles into the groundwater. Heavy metals have been found in the estuary, where the polluted river runs into the sea. In a 2002 report issued by an independent American environmental consulting company (and paid for by the gold company and its partner), the river and wetlands were called "unsuitable for aquatic life."

- Water that is used for heap leaching operations at the Yanacocha mine in Peru is also needed by the local residents for drinking, bathing, and raising livestock. Due to mining activity, the streams have dried up, become laden with sediment, or smell bad. Tens of thousands of fish have perished in the region. At least one lake is contaminated with cyanide, and one stream is acidic. Billions of tons of rock have been heaped into piles that leak acids and heavy metals into surface and ground water.

- More than 1,000 Peruvian peasants were poisoned when a truck from an American company spilled 330 pounds (150 kg) of mercury over 25 miles (40 km) of road. Plans to expand the mine responsible for the spill were successfully stopped in response to protests by the peasants.

While many mining companies bring in schools, medical services, money for social programs, and sometimes jobs, they damage people's ability to live in their traditional ways by damaging their land and water. Communities are now becoming savvier and are demanding a greater financial share of the wealth from the mining companies.

WRAP-UP

Mining has large environmental consequences. Mining produces pollutants such as heavy metals and acids that may leak from the mine site into the environment. Large quantities of fossil fuels are used in mining processes, such as smelting, that also cause pollution. Gold mining is tremendously damaging due to the enormous quantities of waste rock it generates, the water it uses, and the contamination it releases, yet gold is used primarily for ornamental purposes.

After the
Mine Closes

When a mine no longer contains valuable minerals, the land may be restored to health depending on the age of the mine, the financial health of the mining company, and the mine's location. Most mines in the United States that were abandoned before 1977 have not been cleaned up. Abandoned mines are among the most toxic waste sites in the world. This chapter discusses what happens after a mine closes.

MINING REGULATIONS

Laws governing hard rock mining in the United States have changed very little since the Mining Act of 1872. The act was designed to encourage the settlement and development of the western United States and has little relevance in the modern world. Currently, when valuable deposits are found on public lands, mining companies pay no royalties to the federal government. If the company acquires permission to mine, it pays only the 1872 price of $5 an acre. The law contains no provisions for environmental protection. Subsequent amendments have modified the act in only small ways.

The Surface Mining Control and Reclamation Act of 1977 requires that mining sites be restored to their original condition. Under the terms of this act, before a mining operation begins, mine operators must submit plans for restoring the land and for controlling acid mine drainage after the mine is abandoned. All active mining operations pay a tax on their commodity, which then goes into the Abandoned Mine Reclamation Fund. Additionally, many mining states have their own regulations. New Mexico law is especially stringent: It requires all hard rock mines to be reclaimed to a self-sustaining ecosystem. The state will assist financially, but only after the reclamation is complete, to be sure that the job gets done.

Other federal laws are relevant to mining operations, although they do not specifically regulate mining. The Clean Air Act of 1970 governs the emissions from smelters by establishing air quality standards. For example, a smelter must use pollution-reducing technologies so that it does not exceed emissions limits. The Clean Water Act of 1972 (amended in 1977) regulates the type and quantity of pollutants that are discharged into waterways. The Endangered Species Act of 1973 protects all plants and animals living in the area of the mine that are threatened with extinction.

Many mines that were operating before these environmental laws took effect have become environmental nightmares. **Superfund**, formally known as the Comprehensive Environmental Response, Compensation, and Liability Act (CERCLA) of 1980, was created to handle these sites. Superfund is a federal program designated to clean up hazardous waste sites. This law mandates that the federal government respond to releases, or threatened releases, of hazardous substances. If no responsible party can be identified, the government assigns liability and uses the money collected in a trust fund from the petroleum and chemical industries for cleanup. The act mandates the removal of contaminated materials and the implementation of a long-term remedial action plan.

AFTER MINING ENDS

All mines eventually close and leave behind land that has been altered and polluted. Since the passage of the Surface Mining Control and Reclamation Act in 1977, mining companies are required to reclaim the lands that they mine, at least in the United States. But many of the mines that were active in the years before the act were simply abandoned.

When the act was passed in 1977, the country had millions of acres of abandoned mine sites, including 1.1 million acres (4,450 sq. km) of abandoned coal mines alone. Some of these sites have since been reclaimed, but communities continue to suffer from the problems associated with unreclaimed sites. These sites scar the landscape and are used as illegal trash dumps, making them even more of an eyesore. Several children have died in accidents while exploring and playing in abandoned mines. Acid runoff and sediment pollution contaminate municipal water supplies in both rural and urban areas—problems that drive up the costs of water treatment. While it is useful, the Abandoned Mine Reclamation Fund has proved inadequate to address the problems caused by all the abandoned mine sites in the country.

Some companies may be unable to afford the cost of cleaning up their property if the price of gold falls too low. A profitable gold deposit in the Little Rock Mountains of Northeastern Montana was abandoned in 1996 when the price of gold fell so low that mining it was no longer economical. Subsequently, the mine generated acid mine waste that mixed with cyanide derived from the leach operation. The $100 million cost for cleanup was borne by the residents of Montana. This event led to the passing in 1988 of a state initiative that banned cyanide mining.

BUTTE, MONTANA: PORTRAIT OF A SUPERFUND SITE

The most extreme case of mining contamination is in Butte, Montana, which is now the largest Superfund site in the nation. From the moment gold was spotted along Silver Bow Creek in 1864, until the Berkeley open pit was shut down in 1982, Butte was a hard rock mining town. Today, Butte has slightly more than 30,000 residents, but at the peak of copper production, the population was as high as 100,000. In all, some 20 billion pounds (9 billion kg) of copper were stripped from the rock. The mining took place in immense underground shafts until 1960, when the digging of the Berkeley Pit began. Approximately one billion tons (900 million metric tons) of material was removed from the pit, which grew to be one mile (1.6 km) wide, one-half mile (0.8 km) long, and more than one-quarter mile (0.4 km) deep. Ultimately, the pit swallowed about one-third of the town.

When mining ceased, so did the pumping that had once kept groundwater from seeping into the shafts and pits. Twenty-eight billion gallons (106 billion liters) of water per day enters the Berkeley Pit, where it is turned acidic (pH 2.3) by the pit's sulfide rock. Heavy metals also contaminate the water, making the Berkeley Pit a 600-acre (2.4 sq. km) toxic lake. In 1995, more than 300 migrating snow geese died in the pit's water, most likely due to the acid. (Oddly, the pit is also a major tourist attraction.) Other toxic ponds and mountains of contaminated waste rock are located nearby. The groundwater aquifer running beneath Butte is tainted with heavy metals, including lead, cadmium, and copper. Silver Bow Creek runs orange from cyanide, while other nearby surface streams contain dangerous concentrations of arsenic, manganese, lead, copper, and zinc. Lead and arsenic contaminate the soil around the town. Toxic metals are found in the Milltown Reservoir, more than 100 miles (160 km) downstream.

In 1986, the entire floodplain from the Berkeley Pit to the Milltown Reservoir was declared a Superfund site. This site covers about 26 miles (42 km) of stream and streamside habitat. The most polluted of the waterways, Silver Bow Creek and Warm Springs Ponds, received mine, industrial, and municipal wastes for more than a hundred years. Heavy-metal-laden waste rock has been dumped along the creek, and the metals have flowed out over the entire flood plain. Groundwater, surface water, and soils are contaminated with arsenic, copper, zinc, cadmium, lead, and other heavy metals. The waterways no longer

The Berkeley Pit open pit copper mine, filled with water. The highly toxic lake is part of the Silver Bow Creek / Butte Area Superfund site in Montana. *(Rob Crandall / The Image Works)*

support healthy aquatic ecosystems, and fish have been poisoned. When people come into direct contact with tainted water or soil, they wind up ingesting poisoned water or inhaling contaminated air.

Cleaning up Butte has been, and will continue to be, an enormous job. Contaminated waste rock has been placed behind armored, reinforced beams and capped. To keep wildlife from the contaminated habitat, clean ponds and wetlands have been constructed. In November 2003, a water treatment facility began treating and diverting much of the surface water that would have flowed into Berkeley Pit. When the water in the pit reaches a certain height, in about 2018, the plant will begin treating water in the lake. To keep Butte from becoming a toxic wetland, by 2021 pumping will begin to keep the water level down. As the water is pumped, its pH will be neutralized and the metals drawn out. This will create a toxic sludge that will need to be disposed of safely. If the pumping is ever stopped, toxic lake water will flow out over the entire region.

So far, the cleanup efforts have paid off. Much of the water is now cleaner, and the ponds are normally within EPA standards for safe water. The aquatic system and wetlands are currently healthy enough to treat some of the toxic water themselves. A stream bypass of the contaminated region now supports some fish and aquatic insects. Amazingly, new species of fungus and bacteria have been found in the harsh conditions of the pit. These microorganisms produce toxic compounds that have been found to kill cancer cells.

RECLAMATION

A former mine or any other disturbed region that is transformed into a useful landscape—a productive ecosystem, a building site, or a strawberry field, for example—is considered to have been reclaimed. Mine reclamation requires the placement of waste rock in pits that are stabilized, capped, and graded, with soil and vegetation added on top. In some reclaimed mines, a habitat is established for threatened or **endangered species**. For example, the Mesquite Mine of Southern California has established a protection program and a management area for the threatened desert tortoise.

The McLaughlin Mine, located 70 miles (110 km) north of San Francisco near the Napa wine country, is one mining reclamation success story. This site was mined for mercury beginning in 1862. Although the mercury miners knew that gold was present, it was mostly disseminated and at the time was of little value. But as the price of gold went up, and mining techniques were modernized, a company called Homestake Mining showed an interest in the property. The region had suffered so much damage from its years as a mercury mine that one observer described the area as being nearly a moonscape.

Homestake began open-pit gold mining in 1985, after six years of research and engineering plans. Because of the environmental leanings of the local population, the project was under intense scrutiny from the beginning. While mining for gold, the company cleaned up three abandoned mercury mines and began reclamation of their own disturbances—activities that they continued even after the gold was mined out. Soil stripped from the area was saved for revegetation, and erosion was controlled. The company built a freshwater reservoir that created a new habitat for the region's wildlife, including waterfowl, deer, small mammals, mountain lions (*Puma concolor*), bears, coyotes (*Canus latrans*), foxes (*Vulpes sp.*), and raptors. In 1992, the University of California, Davis, established the area as a natural reserve, which the university administers as part of its natural reserve system. The land is studied and used as a classroom as it continues its recovery. The success of this project shows how important planning is to a reclamation effort.

WRAP-UP

Mineral resources are extremely important to modern society, and mining will continue as a human activity for a long time. What happened at Butte, Montana, is an example of the enormous amount of environmental devastation mining can cause and the consequences of pursuing an economic activity without preparing for the long-term impacts. Many mine sites in developing nations are being similarly damaged because environmental regulations are often slack or nonexistent. By contrast, the site of California's McLaughlin Mine is in better shape than it was before gold was mined. To minimize the environmental and social impacts of mining, mining companies should plan for the future financially and environmentally. In developing nations, it is important for companies to protect the livelihoods of the local people.

PART FOUR

POWER GENERATION

Power from Nonrenewable Resources

The following two chapters look at how energy is used in modern society. They also describe the different types of power generation and their influence on land use, pollution, and other concerns. This chapter deals specifically with fossil fuels and nuclear energy.

TYPES OF ENERGY

Some energy sources—solar, wind, hydro, biomass, and geothermal—are considered renewable. For an energy source to be renewable, it must be able to be replaced so rapidly that it does not run out: For example, sunlight used for solar power is soon followed by more sunlight. Other energy sources are nonrenewable. While these energy sources may be replenished, it is not on timescales that are relevant for humans. Fossil fuels, for example, may be forming inside the crust now, but thousands or millions of years will pass before they could become useful resources for humans.

An additional difference between these two power types is in how they make use of land. Nonrenewable energy resources such as petroleum, coal, or uranium for nuclear power plants must be mined or pumped from under the ground, while renewable energy sources such as wind, solar, and biomass must be collected over large expanses of land. Each energy type requires a certain type of landscape: For example, fossil fuels require geological landscapes where economically valuable amounts of the fuels can form; wind farms must be situated in areas that are prone to strong and steady wind; growing biomass requires fertile soil and available water; geothermal energy requires hot rock at or near the Earth's surface.

ENERGY USE

Energy may be used directly, as in a solar-powered oven for cooking food, or it may be converted into a more usable form, such as electricity. However, energy conversion is not very efficient: The more transformations an energy source undergoes before it reaches a useful form, the less energy is available for use. For example, converting solar radiation to plant biomass and then to liquid fuel for driving a car makes use of only a small percentage of the solar energy that was initially absorbed by that plant.

To be really useful, an energy source must be available at all times of day and in all seasons of the year. A solar oven can be used only on a sunny day, but a gas oven can be used as long as the gas tank is not empty. A useful energy source must also be able to be stored. Solar energy is available only when the Sun is out, but biomass stores solar energy for use days, months, or years later, and fossil fuels store solar energy for thousands or millions of years. However, humans can also build power plants and other facilities that can store solar and other types of energy until it is needed.

Mostly, people use energy sources in two forms: As electricity to heat houses and run computers and as liquid fuel to power internal-combustion engines such as those used in cars. To generate electricity, energy is harnessed to heat water that will create steam in a steam-electric power plant. The steam then turns a turbine that is connected to a generator, which supplies the electricity. Steam-electric plants can be powered by fossil fuels or any other type of energy that can heat water, including nuclear, geothermal, or solar energy. Because these plants rely on boiling water, they must be located near large bodies of water for cooling.

FOSSIL FUELS

Modern society is extremely dependent on fossil fuels, which are by far the most commonly used energy source today. Coal, petroleum, and natural gas currently provide about 85% of the world's energy and account for more than 70% of the energy consumed in the United States. The world's energy consumption is growing, mostly in the use of fossil fuels. Between 1950 and 2004, the use of oil increased 8-fold, coal increased 2.6-fold, and natural gas increased 14-fold, for a 523% total increase in fossil fuel use.

Fossil fuels have many advantages: They are readily available, plentiful, easily recovered, and easily stored. Fossil fuels are also comparatively inexpensive and relatively concentrated: A small amount of fuel can generate a large amount of power. The technologies and machines that developed with fossil fuels are long established and widespread. Gasoline remains especially important because it is one of the few energy sources available as a liquid and can be used in cars and trucks. Natural gas is used for home heating and cooking, and it fuels electrical generating plants.

Fossil fuels are located in rock at or beneath the land surface, including offshore areas. Coal is collected by hard-rock mining. To retrieve oil or gas, a drilling rig penetrates a hole through the overlying rock into an underground reservoir and then pumps the fuels from the ground. Oil wells can be drilled vertically, horizontally, or subhorizontally. Oil lying under an environmentally sensitive area can be tapped by a rig located outside that area. Natural gas may be found

An active oil rig on the prairie. *(Andrew Penner / iStockphoto)*

floating on the heavier crude in a petroleum deposit, or it may migrate into a separate reservoir. Natural gas is cleaner and more energy efficient than petroleum and does not need to be refined, which makes it less expensive than oil.

In 2006, Steven E. Koonin, chief scientist of British Petroleum, suggested that there may be 40 years of proven oil reserves at current production rates and possibly another 40 years that are as yet undiscovered. Natural gas has about 70 years proven and possibly another 70 to be discovered. Coal has 160 years proven and probably at least six times as much yet to be discovered. If needed, new technologies could harness lower grade coal or coal waste that previously had been considered unusable.

Because conventionally used fossil fuels—oil, coal, and natural gas—are limited and often difficult to control politically, energy companies are looking to other sources of fossil fuels. **Oil shale** is rock that contains oil that is dispersed through it and has not collected in reservoirs. Oil shale is currently mined in open pits. To release the fuel from oil shale, the rock is crushed and heated to between 840°F and 930°F (450°C and 500°C) and then washed with enormous amounts of water. This process converts the fuel to petroleum, which then can be extracted from the rock. The amount of fuel that is available as oil shale is estimated to be comparable to the amount remaining in conventional oil reserves.

The United States contains 60% to 70% of the world's oil shale, most of it located in Wyoming, Utah, and Colorado. These oil shale resources underlie a total area of 16,000 square miles (40,000 km), a little less than the combined area of Massachusetts and New Hampshire. Mining such an enormous area would potentially be devastating to the environment. In addition, environmental restoration over such large areas is difficult and expensive. Estonia, Australia, Germany, Israel, and Jordan also have significant oil shale deposits.

Tar sands are rocky materials mixed with very thick oil. Because this tar is too thick to pump, tar sands are strip-mined. Separating the soil from the rocky material requires processing with hot water and caustic soda, to create a slurry. Shaking this slurry causes the oil to float to the top, where it can be skimmed. Tar sands represent as much as 66% of the world's total reserves of oil. About 75% of these reserves are in Alberta, Canada, and in Venezuela. Mining tar sands destroys the landscape. In Canada that would involve the degradation of boreal forests, wetlands, and river systems.

Producing oil from oil shale or tar sands creates an enormous amount of waste rock. Processing the rock uses a tremendous amount of energy and water. This is especially problematic in the oil shale deposits of the United States, which happen to be located in arid areas. Extracting usable energy from oil shale and tar sands produces much more greenhouse gas than does processing the same amount of conventional oil—four times as much in the case of tar sands.

Fossil fuels send an enormous amount of pollution into the air and water. They also release greenhouse gases into the atmosphere, which cause global warming. Since the end of the Industrial Revolution, when fossil-fuel use became widespread, the global temperature has risen 1.8°F (1°C). Temperatures have jumped noticeably since the 1990s, and fossil fuel use has climbed even more.

NUCLEAR POWER

Nuclear fission plants, the only type of nuclear power plant that has so far been developed on a large scale, create their energy from enriched uranium. Because uranium must be mined, and its supply is limited, nuclear power is considered nonrenewable. If fossil fuels were replaced by nuclear fission, current estimates surmise that there would be only enough uranium for about 6 to 30 years, although uranium can theoretically be collected from seawater. Research is ongoing into breeder reactors, in which the byproducts of nuclear fission are made to breed new fuel, and into nuclear fusion, which has the potential to produce unlimited clean power.

Power from nuclear fission is clean and efficient but has many problems. The plants generate much more waste heat than do coal-fired power plants. They need to be near a water source for cooling, which creates thermal pollution. Accidents also are a potential problem: The 1979 partial core meltdown at the Three Mile Island nuclear plant in Pennsylvania and the 1986 explosion and meltdown at Chernobyl, Ukraine (at that time part of the USSR), caused several European countries to abandon the use of nuclear power entirely and prompted the United States and countries in other parts of Europe to halt the construction of new nuclear power plants. The biggest problem associated with nuclear power plants is waste disposal. Long-lived radioactive wastes remain a potential danger for more than 10,000 years. (Nuclear waste issues are described in detail in Chapter 17.)

People in the nuclear power industry say that new designs reduce the chances for catastrophic accidents such as meltdowns, but opponents respond that the danger of human failure remains high. Concerns about global warming are causing a resurgence of interest in nuclear power because nuclear plants burn cleanly and produce no greenhouse gases. Right now, the United States gets just over 20% of its electricity from nuclear power plants, at much lower operational costs than fossil-fuel plants.

Recent discussions about renewing the development of nuclear energy are controversial. Although nuclear energy does not cause global warming, the technology has many problems. Besides the history of nuclear power plant accidents, many people may be exposd to potentially harmful radiation during the transport of nuclear materials. Also, nuclear energy creates radioactive waste, which must be safely stored for more than 10,000 years. Proponents say that the dangers have lessened as technologies have improved and that the damage being done to the planet by fossil fuels makes nuclear power more attractive.

WRAP-UP

For many reasons—environmental, political, and social—the world will need to shift its tremendous reliance on fossil fuels to other sources. The environmental reasons include global warming, pollution, and the environmental damage caused by extracting these resources. The political reasons include the instability of the locations where the remaining supplies of fossil fuels are now concentrated, primarily the Middle East. Socially, relying on fossil fuels is risky because they are nonrenewable and unsustainable. The shift away from fossil fuels must be done gradually, but also as quickly as possible, and must lead to clean, sustainable power sources that are suited to a particular location. Many of these renewable energy sources will be discussed in the following chapter.

Power from Renewable Resources

As supplies of easily accessible fossil fuels diminish, prices rise, scientists continue to assess the damage being done to the Earth system from burning carbon, and politicians begin to listen to the scientists, renewable, alternative energy resources such as geothermal, wind, solar, and biomass are becoming more significant. As this chapter will show, many of these resources come directly or indirectly from the Sun. Solar power harnesses the Sun's radiation, while wind power and hydropower take advantage of how the Sun's energy drives the atmosphere and the water cycle. Biomass taps into the solar energy harnessed by plants during photosynthesis (even fossil fuels are ancient solar energy that was concentrated and stored by long-dead plants). Of course, not all energy sources come from the Sun. Geothermal power utilizes the energy stored in the Earth's hotter underground regions.

SOLAR POWER

The Sun provides an enormous and inexhaustible amount of energy to Earth. Solar radiation can be used as it is, as in a solar oven, or it can be converted into heat or electricity. The heat from solar energy can warm up water in a hot water heater or be used for heating a house. Solar-heated hot water can be stored in insulated tanks so that it is available on cloudy days or at night. Where higher temperatures are needed, the Sun's rays must be concentrated. One method is to carefully align mirrors to focus the sunlight, which can heat water to produce steam and run a generator in a steam electric plant.

Photovoltaic cells convert sunlight directly into electricity. Because these cells generate only a small amount of electricity, they are mostly suitable for powering calculators or watches and for other low power needs. To produce larger amounts of electricity, these cells must be connected into solar batteries. Unfortunately, photovoltaic cells are only about 7% to 11% efficient, and so generating a significant amount of power requires huge arrays of cells. Large-scale solar power collection requires the building of panels, parabolic troughs, thermal dishes, or power towers.

Solar power collectors can be built in what is normally unused space, such as on rooftops, so not as much land is used as with other power sources. For example, meeting one person's daily energy needs in a sunny location requires only about 430 square feet (40 sq. m) of solar collectors, which can easily be built on top of a roof. Another benefit of solar power is that it does not create wastes or pollution.

The potential use for solar energy is enormous, particularly in the Sunbelt (the southwestern United States, where the climate is typically very mild), but so far the cost of collecting, converting, and storing this energy has been high. Solar power is becoming more cost effective as rising energy costs inspire research and development into more efficient solar systems. This, in turn, inspires households and businesses to convert to solar, which brings down prices by the economy of scale. Still, much more can be done to increase solar energy usage.

The uses of solar power described above are called "active" solar because of the way they actively collect the Sun's rays for heat or electricity. A building erected for "passive" solar power captures the Sun's heat through the way it is designed. For example, passive solar houses are built to maximize the collection of heat in the winter and minimize it in the summer by positioning the house and the windows in the best way for both purposes. A passive solar home may use up to one-third less heat in the winter. Solar radiation entering a passive solar building may also heat an insulator, such as a water tank, which can store heat for release at a later time. Heat can be stored for days, or even months, in insulation buried around the building's foundation. In passive solar buildings, fans move heat to where it is needed.

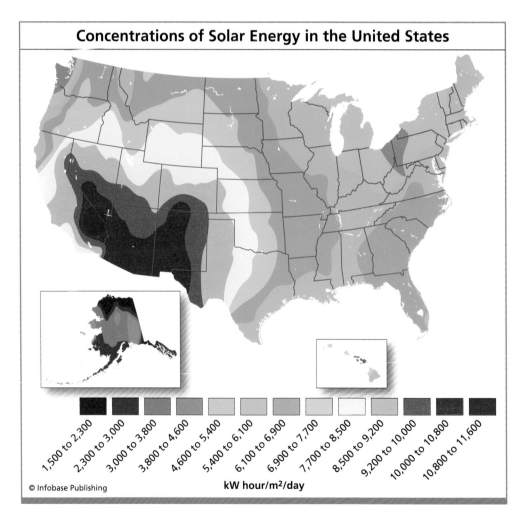

Concentrations of Solar Energy in the United States

1,500 to 2,300 · 2,300 to 3,000 · 3,000 to 3,800 · 3,800 to 4,600 · 4,600 to 5,400 · 5,400 to 6,100 · 6,100 to 6,900 · 6,900 to 7,700 · 7,700 to 8,500 · 8,500 to 9,200 · 9,200 to 10,000 · 10,000 to 10,800 · 10,800 to 11,600

kW hour/m²/day

© Infobase Publishing

The southwestern United States receives enormous amounts of solar energy. This energy could be harnessed and used to power homes and businesses in the region.

WIND POWER

The Sun's energy falls on the Earth unevenly. More of this energy strikes the equator than the poles, for example. When the Sun's rays heat the air, the air becomes warmer and rises, causing nearby air to rush in horizontally to fill the gap. This horizontal air movement creates wind. Only 1% to 3% of the solar energy that reaches the Earth is converted to wind energy, but that number is 50 to 100 times greater than the amount of solar energy that is converted to biomass through photosynthesis.

At this time, wind energy generates about 1% of global power usage. About 70% of that amount is generated in Europe, and 20% in the United States. However, wind power is rapidly growing in popularity: Global use is rising tremendously, with an increase of 41% in 2005 and 32% in 2006. In the United States, wind power usage increased an average of 22% annually between 2002 and 2006. Improvements in technology have brought down the cost of building a wind plant by 80%, and new wind farms on- and offshore are being planned all over the world. This cost reduction is so dramatic that it is now less expensive to build a wind farm than to build any other type of power plant. Although wind energy is still more expensive to generate at this time than fossil fuel or nuclear power, when the entire cost to health and the environment is factored in, wind is extremely competitive.

To create usable power, wind moves turbine blades, which drive a generator that converts the energy into electrical current. Small wind turbines are used in isolated locations, but the large-scale use of wind energy requires a wind farm. Turbines must be spaced far enough apart that they do not compete for wind energy; thus, wind farms can take up a lot of space. The best locations for wind farms are where wind speeds are moderate to high, around 12.5 miles per hour (20 km per hour), and fairly constant, with few large gusts. Mountain ridges or passes, cliff faces, and coastlines are often suitable locations. Wind farms may also be located offshore, although the turbines are easily corroded, making the cost of operating an offshore wind farm higher. Wind is variable in most locations, so wind power must be stored if

Wind turbines spread out on the landscape. *(Craig Hill / Dreamstime.com)*

energy is to be consistently available. This can be done in existing hydroelectric plants or in facilities constructed for the purpose of storage.

Wind has tremendous advantages over other power sources: It is renewable, nonpolluting, and widely available. Unlike fossil fuel and nuclear power plants, wind turbines do not need water for cooling. Land used for wind farms can be put to multiple uses because wind turbines can be placed on agricultural and ranch land and do not individually take up much space. As with any power plant, constructing wind turbines requires material and energy, yet the amount of energy used to create a wind turbine is made up after only 9 months of operation. Over its lifetime, a wind turbine will harness 50 times more energy than was used to build it. When the turbines are removed, the land will recover completely. Besides producing no greenhouse gases, harnessing wind power takes energy from the atmosphere, which offsets some of the heat that is added from greenhouse gas emissions produced by the use of other energy sources.

Wind power has downsides, of course. Carving a wind farm from wilderness would require logging the land and building roads and power lines. Wind farms take up a large amount of land. A wind farm meant to produce the same amount of energy as a conventional power plant would require an area of about 77 square miles (200 sq. km). Wind farms in some locations are unsightly, and the beauty of the mountain passes and coastlines on which they need to be constructed may be marred by the turbines. The need to store wind energy in constructed facilities means added expense and increased land usage for the operation.

One longtime objection to wind power is that the turbines kill birdlife, particularly raptors, which get caught in the turbine blades. Although some wind farms have a higher incidence of dead birds than other nearby areas, a study conducted by the Royal Society for the Protection of Birds in the United Kingdom concluded that wind farms are not a significant hazard if they are carefully placed. The study concluded that the losses of birdlife are more than counteracted by the decrease in global warming that can be attributed to this power source.

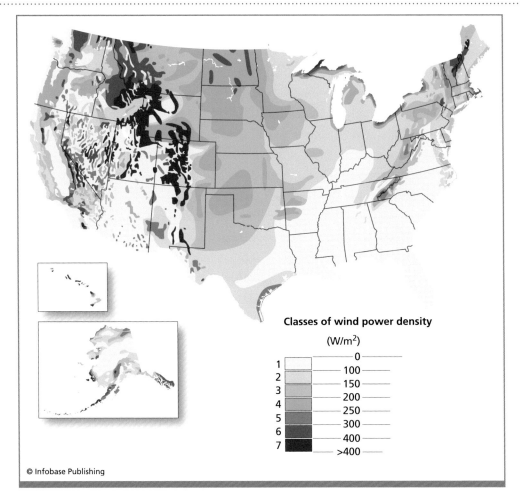

Wind-power density measures the amount of energy that is available at the site for conversion by a wind turbine. Portions of the intermontane west and northern United States have abundant wind energy.

Estimates are that wind power could supply 40 times the current demand for electricity. However, if all turbines were onshore, converting to wind power to supply all of society's electricity would require nearly 13% of the Earth's land area. Offshore wind farms would take up much less space because they can supply about 7 times as much energy in the same amount of area due to the abundant and steady winds.

HYDROPOWER

Water rushing through a narrow opening or cascading down a rock face packs a tremendous amount of energy. This harnessed energy is called hydroelectric power or **hydropower**. Modern hydropower plants harness the kinetic energy of water as it cascades naturally down rock faces such as Niagara Falls, as well as down any one of thousands of dam walls. The falling water spins the blades of a turbine, which powers a generator that produces the electricity.

Hydropower is pollutant free and renewable, as long as streams flow. However, harnessing this power requires altering the landscape by constructing dams across river valleys. Dams also collect the water that rises behind them to form the man-made lakes. Drowning a river valley may bring about the loss of beautiful scenery or cultural artifacts. When a valley is drowned without first clearing out its vegetation, the vegetation rots and creates methane, a potent greenhouse gas, which rises into the atmosphere.

Hydropower plants produce about 24% of the world's electricity. Almost all of the world's major rivers are dammed, most of them in several locations along their routes. Since 1950, the number of large dams over 50 feet (15 m) in height has increased from 5,700 to more than 41,000. In the United States, nearly all the rivers have been dammed. About 2,000 hydropower plants generate 13% of U.S. electricity, a figure estimated to be about 75% of the potential hydropower in the contiguous United States. This is down from 33% in the 1940s. Some countries, such as Norway and Sweden, get nearly 100% of their electricity from hydropower.

Hydropower is unlikely to grow as a source of energy in the developed world because all the major rivers are already dammed, and people want to protect those remaining valleys that would be good dam sites. Many developing nations have greatly untapped hydropower potential, at least some of which will be developed in the future.

BIOFUELS

Living or recently deceased organisms or their metabolic products that can be converted to energy are called **biofuels**. Solar energy is the basis of all biofuels because nearly all plant and animal life gets its energy directly or indirectly from photosynthesis. Biomass can be used directly, as in the burning of wood, charcoal, or manure to cook food or heat homes. Most of the 15% of global energy consumption that biofuels provide is burned in this "low-tech" manner. Usable fuel can also be created from biomass. To do this, the appropriate plants need to be grown, collected, dried, fermented, and burned. In addition, wastes from agriculture, forestry, and households are great sources of material for biofuels.

Biofuels are unique among alternative energy sources because they can be made into liquids that can be burned in internal combustion engines, thereby replacing gasoline. Ethanol is one type of liquid biofuel. It can be produced from biological organisms or from fossil fuels. Biogas is created from rotting biomass. If this process—called gasification—is controlled and conducted at high temperatures, biogas production is more efficient. Another form of engine fuel, biodiesel, is created from crops such as soybeans or rapeseed, animal fat, or waste oils. Biogas can be used instead of natural gas, and biodiesel can replace diesel fuels derived from fossil fuels.

As an alternative energy source, biofuels have a lot of good features. They are renewable and can be stored as biomass or in liquid form. Biofuels are relatively clean, but they are not pollutant free. They produce about 20% to 40% fewer pollutants than fossil fuels. Ethanol produces only CO_2 and water as waste, the same byproducts that are produced when the material is allowed to decompose. Because the CO_2 and water were absorbed by the plants from the atmosphere as they grew, the return of these gases back into the atmosphere has no net effect on atmospheric greenhouse gas levels. (This is not the case with fossil fuels, which return ancient carbon dioxide and other gases to the atmosphere.) Because they are cleaner than fossil fuels, biofuels are added to gasoline in the United States as a supplement.

Biofuels have limits as an alternative fuel source. Even if all the suitable wastes were converted to biofuels, the amount of energy produced would be much less than the amounts of fossil fuels that are used each year. For biofuels to replace a large percentage of fossil fuels, crops would need to be grown for the purpose. Choosing the appropriate crop would be extremely important because different plants produce vastly different amounts of oil. For example, soybeans produce about 40 to 50 U.S. gallons per acre (35,000 to 45,000 l/km); rapeseed produces 110 to 145 gallons per acre (100,000 to 130,000 l/km); palm oil, 650 gallons per acre (580,000 l/km); and algae, 10,000 to 20,000 gallons per acre (9,000,000 to 18,000,000 l/km). Powering U.S. cars with biofuels derived from soybeans, a popular biofuel source, would require devoting twice the land area of the United States to soybean production. Choosing rapeseed, which is used in parts of Europe, would require two-thirds of the land area of the United States.

Malaysia and Indonesia are studying the feasibility of producing energy from palm oil, but this plan has other problems. Clearing land for palm-oil production threatens tropical forests and the rare orangutans and other animals that reside in them. Cutting and burning rain forest trees also releases much more CO_2 into the atmosphere than is taken up by the oil palms.

As was described in Part Two, large-scale, modern agriculture is very hard on the environment. Pesticides, fertilizers, water, and fossil fuels would be needed to produce the enormous amounts of any crops chosen for large-scale conversion to biofuels. In fact, growing these crops would require such large amounts of fossil fuels that there would be little net energy gain. The recent major increase in the size of the Gulf of Mexico dead zone may be attributed to the current push to grow more corn for biofuels. Because of the enormous impact growing crops for fuel would have on the terrestrial and marine environments, many environmentalists do not think that biofuels are a good way to replace fossil fuels.

Algae are the possible exception and may be the best bet for large-scale biofuel production. Replacing all the fuel currently used for transportation in the United States would require only 0.3% of the nation's land area if the crop were the type of algae that contains 50% oil. An additional benefit of algae is that they grow best where there is a lot of solar radiation, making desert lands, where most other crops do not grow well, suitable for the task. The algae could be fed agricultural and other wastes, which would be an efficient recycling of resources. At this time, research into algae biofuel is in the early stages.

GEOTHERMAL

The Earth's interior gets warmer as depth beneath the surface increases. In some locations, such as near active volcanoes, this high internal heat rises to very near the surface. In these regions, hot water may emerge at hot springs or if the hot area is dry, water can be pumped in through a well drilled into the ground. In either case, steam from the hot water can be used to drive a turbine that spins a generator to create electricity.

Geothermal energy is sustainable because the amount of hot rock lying beneath the Earth's surface is unlimited. Geothermal energy is also nonpolluting and does not emit greenhouse gases. However, one

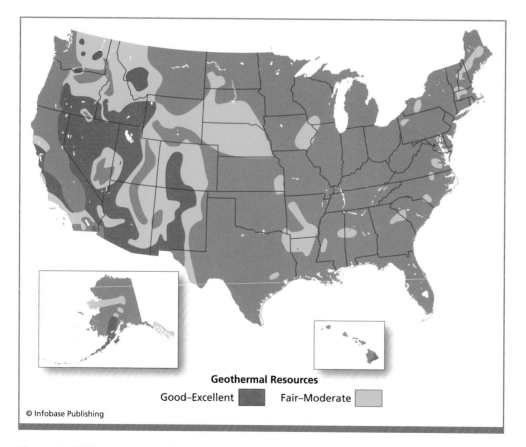

Geothermal Resources

Good–Excellent   Fair–Moderate

© Infobase Publishing

The potential for geothermal energy in the United States is highest in the West.

possible downside to geothermal energy is that it is usually found in volcanic regions, which are often scenic. Construction of geothermal plants could degrade the natural beauty of some locations.

Geothermal energy is used extensively in Iceland, which gets about 17% of its electricity and 87% of its domestic heating and hot water supply from geothermal sources. In the United States, production of geothermal energy is about one-third of the global total: Enough geothermal energy is produced annually to meet the electrical needs of more than one million people. The Department of Energy estimates that geothermal sources could provide up to 30 times the current annual electrical energy use of the United States. The most favorable geothermal sites are located in California and the Rocky Mountain states.

The world's largest dry steam geothermal field is the Geysers in northern California. (A **geyser** is a hot spring that periodically shoots steam and hot water into the air.) Treated sewage effluent from nearby cities is injected into the hot rock to create steam, instead of being dumped into nearby rivers and streams. Not only is this effluent being kept out of the water supply, but it is assisting in providing a renewable source of energy for about one million people.

WRAP-UP

It is unlikely that any single source of energy will be used in the future to supply all or even most of the energy needs for human activities. For instance, homes located in the Sunbelt could convert to solar power, while every field in the U.S. Midwest could turn to wind turbines. Biofuel waste could power at least some of the cars and trucks in the corn- and soybean-growing states. These changes are unlikely to come from the energy companies themselves; they will be made when the government mandates the efficient use of energy and consumers demand alternative energy sources.

PART FIVE

URBAN AREAS

Urbanization

The final step in land development is **urbanization**, a process that occurs as population density in an area increases. As an urban area grows, the total land area it covers gets larger, and the concentration of roads, buildings, and other structures increases. This chapter discusses how urbanization eats away at natural landscapes and farmland by converting them to cities and suburbs. Paving over farmland often means losing the land with the best soils, which compromises the ability of a region or nation to grow food for its people. Urban areas also generate pollution of the air, water, and land. Cities in developed nations are somewhat protected by antipollution laws. However, in many developing nations, pollution regulations and enforcement are nearly nonexistent.

THE GROWTH OF CITIES

For most of human history, people lived in small groups or tribes. Cities of more than 100,000 residents first arose in ancient times. At its peak, ancient Rome covered nearly 4 square miles (10 sq. km) and had more than 800,000 inhabitants. Beautifully constructed aqueducts carried drinking water into the city from the hills as far as 44 miles (70 km) away. Food and other goods came into the city largely down rivers and from across seas.

With a few notable exceptions, large cities became common only during the population explosion of the past three centuries. In 1800, less than 3% of the world's population lived in cities of 20,000 or more (at that time, London was the world's largest city, with about 1 million people). As mechanization during the Industrial Revolution made growing and transporting food easier, farm families that were no longer needed on the land flocked into the cities looking for work. The new factories needed the large labor force, and the prospect of jobs brought even more people into the cities. As population density increased, the air became polluted with smoke, the streams filled with sewage (which backed up into the streets), and waterborne diseases such as cholera became a fact of life.

The number of urban dwellers has increased rapidly in the past several decades throughout the world: The urban population totaled 25% in the mid-1960s, 40% by 1980, and 47% in 2000. By 2030, 60% of the world's people are expected to be living in cities. Most of these increases in urban population have occurred in the developing nations; the transition from rural to urban life took place earlier in the twentieth century in the developed nations.

Urban areas with more than 10 million inhabitants are known as megacities. Between 1950 and 2005, the number of megacities expanded from just one (the New York metropolitan area) to 20.

Megalopolises appear to be the next wave of urbanization. In extensively populated regions, megacities merge, resulting in the urbanization of an entire region. A megalopolis is growing in the eastern United States, where Boston, Massachusetts, and Washington, D.C., are forming the northern and southern points of a vast urban area that includes Providence, Rhode Island; New Haven, Connecticut; New York City; Newark, New Jersey; Philadelphia, Pennsylvania; and Baltimore, Maryland. Similar megalopolises are forming that link the cities of Tokyo,

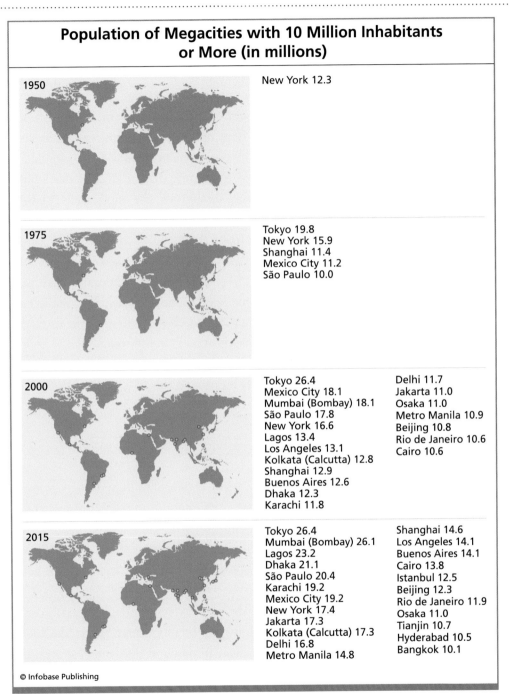

Population of Megacities with 10 Million Inhabitants or More (in millions)

1950
New York 12.3

1975
Tokyo 19.8
New York 15.9
Shanghai 11.4
Mexico City 11.2
São Paulo 10.0

2000
Tokyo 26.4
Mexico City 18.1
Mumbai (Bombay) 18.1
São Paulo 17.8
New York 16.6
Lagos 13.4
Los Angeles 13.1
Kolkata (Calcutta) 12.8
Shanghai 12.9
Buenos Aires 12.6
Dhaka 12.3
Karachi 11.8
Delhi 11.7
Jakarta 11.0
Osaka 11.0
Metro Manila 10.9
Beijing 10.8
Rio de Janeiro 10.6
Cairo 10.6

2015
Tokyo 26.4
Mumbai (Bombay) 26.1
Lagos 23.2
Dhaka 21.1
São Paulo 20.4
Karachi 19.2
Mexico City 19.2
New York 17.4
Jakarta 17.3
Kolkata (Calcutta) 17.3
Delhi 16.8
Metro Manila 14.8
Shanghai 14.6
Los Angeles 14.1
Buenos Aires 14.1
Cairo 13.8
Istanbul 12.5
Beijing 12.3
Rio de Janeiro 11.9
Osaka 11.0
Tianjin 10.7
Hyderabad 10.5
Bangkok 10.1

© Infobase Publishing

One feature of urbanization today is the continuing trend of ever-larger metropolitan areas.

Osaka, and Kyoto in Japan, and London and the Midlands cities in Great Britain.

In megacities like New York, land is incredibly expensive or virtually nonexistent. Therefore, the only direction the city can expand is upward, by building skyscrapers. Skyscrapers maximize the use of a small piece of land by piling floor upon floor of living or commercial space into the sky. This stacking of people has resulted in a population density for all five boroughs of New York City of 27,228 per square mile (10,292 per sq. km). For Manhattan, the city's most densely populated borough, the population density is 66,940 per square mile (25,850 per sq. km). By contrast, the population density of Fargo, North Dakota, is 2,388 per square mile (922 per sq. km).

In most cities, development is mixed. Housing, shopping, and businesses can be found in the same neighborhood or nearby: People may live above a clothing store, shop at the corner market, and work two subway stops away. Public transportation is well developed, and people walk or use buses and light rail to get around. Many city residents do not own cars or use them only to escape the city, rather than to get around within it.

SUBURBS

Suburbs grow in rings around cities. Their population density is lower than a city's, with many single-family homes and few buildings above two stories high. Where land is inexpensive, growth is outward, rather than upward. Suburbanites depend on various means of transportation, such as a well-developed highway system or light rail, to commute into cities for work.

In many parts of the world, the poorest city dwellers live in the suburbs, while the wealthy people live in the city center, where the social and cultural activities are greatest. In much of the United States, the opposite is true: Middle-class and affluent people have moved out to the suburbs in search of larger homes, abandoning the inner cities to the poor. Some newer cities, such as those in the Sunbelt, have very little city center; they are mostly suburbs.

Cities are getting larger not only because population is growing, but also because people are demanding larger houses that take up more space. Larger houses also require more natural resources to build and maintain and more energy per person to run. In addition, there are more houses needed per family. Multiple generational households, which had been the norm for many centuries, are no longer common. Divorce creates a family of two households where once there was only one.

In a 2005 study, researchers from Michigan State University found that in countries where biodiversity is particularly at risk, such as China, between 1985 and 2000, the number of households grew annually by 3.1%, but the population increased only 1.8%. The number of residents per household dropped from 7.7 to 4.0 during that same time. Had the larger statistic remained, there would have been 155 million fewer households. These additional households contribute to deforestation, which, for example, impacts the bamboo forests that are home to China's last giant pandas.

Ground surfaces in suburban areas are not the same as in natural landscapes. Along with paved surfaces and buildings, the dominant plant life in suburbs is lawns. Because these individual plots of greenery are usually created from grasses that are not native to the area, they require a lot of fertilizers and water to maintain, particularly in the arid West, where plants can evaporate as much as 1 inch (2.2 cm) of water per week.

A 2005 study by Cristina Milesi at the National Aeronautic and Space Administration's (NASA) Ames Research Center in California found that the total amount of lawn in the country is about 49,400 square miles (128,000 sq. km), slightly more than the area of the state of North Carolina. There is three times more land covered with lawn than with irrigated corn, making lawn the single largest irrigated crop in the country. If all of this lawn is well watered (which it is not), Milesi estimates that about 200 gallons (760 l) of drinking-quality water per person per day would be necessary to maintain it. Because aquifers are being used unsustainably, and populations in arid regions are exploding, in some areas of the country this could be interpreted as a misuse of water resources.

In the United States, 19,000 square miles (49,000 sq. km) of rural cropland and wilderness were developed between 1982 and 1992, the equivalent of covering half of Ohio with a subdivision. Each year, more than one million new single-family homes and more than 10,000 miles (16,000 km) of new roads are built. Some people derogatorily call the spread of urban environments across the landscape urban sprawl. Sprawl is low-density development characterized by strip malls and subdivisions. In these areas, land is zoned for a single use—housing, industrial, commercial—therefore, the activities that make up a person's daily life are located some distance apart. A car is virtually essential for commuting to work, shopping, attending church, and other daily activities.

Sprawl that extends well outward from the city center is known as an exurb. As the land nearest the city center is built up, developers go

Suburban sprawl around Las Vegas, Clark County, Nevada. *(Lynn Betts / Natural Resources Conservation Service)*

even farther out, where land is less expensive. In the exurbs, houses are larger, roads are wider, and big-box stores with expansive parking lots are even more common. Residents of exurbs may live, work, attend school, and engage in all of their social, cultural, and community activities outside of the city center.

The Phoenix, Arizona, metropolitan area has a population density of about 223 people per square mile (86 per sq. km), although population density in the city of Phoenix is much higher, at 2,782 per square mile (1,074 per sq. km). The buildings are only one or two stories high and are separated by lawns, gardens, and, of course, roads and parking lots. Lawns in Phoenix are especially poorly adapted because the region is very dry and gets most of its water from rivers outside the area. Nonetheless, the Phoenix area now sports more than 200 golf courses, which require not only a large amount of water, but also fertilizer and weed killers. Growth is rampant. Between 1996 and 2005, the city grew by 37%, with much of the growth taking place in the exurbs.

URBANIZATION OF FARMLAND

Covering up land with concrete, asphalt, and other impermeable surfaces greatly reduces a region's primary productivity. Photosynthetic productivity in rainy environments can be reduced by as much as 20 days per year as natural landscapes are replaced by roads, houses, and commercial and industrial structures. (The opposite is true in arid and semiarid conditions, where the addition of water to the land in gardens and lawns increases productivity.) Productivity is also lost if farmland is replaced by city surfaces, although typically not as much.

Agricultural advances have forced people to move from farms into cities looking for work. As cities grow, sprawl paves over farmland because some of the same features that make good-quality farmland— flat land, good soil, access to water, and temperate climate—are also features that are desirable in cities. As farmlands are lost, their soils are paved over. When this happens, it is difficult or impossible to bring that soil back to its former quality.

Marc Imhoff, a biologist at NASA's Goddard Space Flight Center, has tried to quantify the amount and quality of farmland that is being lost to urbanization. Determining how much farmland is being lost is difficult, but Imhoff realized that the lights that appear on detailed satellite images of Earth at night would reveal how much land has been urbanized. Imhoff superimposed a map of soil quality onto a map of urbanization that he made from the satellite images. The quality of a soil was assigned based on limiting factors, which might include wetness that must be drained or acidity that must be limed before farming. The more limiting factors a soil had, Imhoff reasoned, the more expensive and difficult it would be to farm. Soils with no limiting factors are perfect, while prime soils, the next level down, have three or fewer limiting factors.

Imhoff's study of the United States revealed that soils with six or more limiting factors were the least likely to be urbanized. This is not surprising, as these lands tend to be in deserts or on mountains that are not easily developed (although desert cities have certainly grown since the advent of central air conditioning). Imhoff also found that soils with no limiting factors were less likely to be urbanized (about 3%), which he speculates is because these soils are being protected. The most likely soils to be urbanized were prime soils, with one or two limiting factors: About 5% of those soils have been urbanized.

"The impacts [of soil loss] on production are variable, but they're generally negative. And the impacts may be disproportional to the area converted," Imhoff states, in the article "Urbanization's Aftermath" that was posted on the Goddard Earth Observing System (EOS) Web site in 2002. "So while only three percent of the land area in the United States is urbanized," he adds, "that three percent used to be the most productive soils we had."

California provides an example of the urbanization of farmland. The state is the largest agricultural economy in the United States by far, producing half of all of the nation's fruits, nuts, and vegetables each year. Despite the importance of California's agriculture to the food supply and to the state's economy, no effort is being made to

A satellite image of Earth indicates regions that have undergone urbanization. *(NASA)*

preserve the state's richest soils. Sixteen percent has already been lost to urbanization, and many more of the state's best soils are in urbanization's path. Between 1984 and 1992, California lost 3% of its total cropland—enough land to grow grain to feed 45 million people—and each year, nearly 100,000 more acres (400 sq. km) of California farmland are permanently converted to nonfarming uses. One of the world's most agriculturally rich areas is California's Central Valley, which produces 8% of the country's food. By 2040, the Central Valley will become home to nearly 12 million people—double the 2005 population. Imhoff's fear is that more than 50% of the state's best soils may be lost in the next few decades.

The United States is not currently at risk of having people go hungry due to farmland losses, but because arable soils may be lost in other ways (for example, by erosion), these losses may put future generations at risk of being unable to grow enough food. In developing nations, losses of agricultural productivity may be felt more immediately. The worst case may be Egypt, which has all of its arable land on the Nile Delta, where the rapidly growing population is forced to live because the alternative is to move into the inhospitable Sahara Desert. China is also urbanizing some of its best farmland.

WRAP-UP

Worldwide, human flight toward large urban areas is boosting the urban population upward three times faster than the general population growth. This mass movement to the cities has caused urban areas to expand at a rapid rate. In developing nations, much of the move from a rural to a city lifestyle is due to the difficulty of farmers making a living on the land. Urban areas in some parts of the United States, particularly in the Sun Belt, have been rapidly expanding as urban sprawl. These expansions take place at the expense of wild lands and farmland, which will likely someday be needed. If there were large-scale land-use planning, city planners would move to urbanize the poorer quality soils—those that are rocky, sloped, or arid—rather than prime soils needed for farming. As Imhoff states, "Humans tend to congregate where the best resources are. Is it wise to take the best soils and turn them into parking lots?"

Environmental Effects of Urbanization

Urban areas are extremely polluting: In some cases, they create more pollution than agricultural land. This chapter discusses how cities affect the air, water, land, and even climate of the region where they are located. Urban pollution spreads well beyond the cities, affecting farmland and wild lands in the vicinity. Some of the pollutants generated in cities move around the Earth. Air pollutants cause acid rain or contribute to global warming, while water pollutants travel downstream into rivers, lakes, and the oceans.

CITIES AND WATER POLLUTION

Cities pollute waterways in several ways, including directly dumping sewage and chemical waste, allowing runoff from impermeable surfaces such as parking lots, and producing air pollutants that become smog or fall as rain. Once pollutants enter the water, they flow through streams, ponds, lakes, and into the groundwater. Many pollutants ultimately end up in the oceans.

Human populations have long dumped their waste directly into nearby waterways, which were able to absorb the waste. But with the large increases in population densities and the increasing toxicity of waste, the waterways are no longer able to absorb the waste and therefore become polluted. Because water evaporates, but pollutants do not, many toxic chemicals become concentrated and more dangerous. Organic pollutants, which make up the largest volume of waste, are **biodegradable**: They can be broken down by bacteria into stable, nontoxic, inorganic compounds, such as carbon dioxide (CO_2), water (H_2O), and ammonia. Organic material acts as fertilizer in an ecosystem: The addition of large amounts of waste causes the bacteria population to explode. **Aerobic** bacteria, which need oxygen, consume the waste until the oxygen runs out. **Anaerobic** bacteria, which do not need oxygen, then degrade the waste further, producing the byproducts hydrogen sulfide (the rotten egg smell of rotting waste) and methane. Compounds that are not biodegradable may break apart or become ionized, dissolve, or combine with other chemicals to form new compounds, some of which are also hazardous. Pollutants may also attach to sediments and fall to the bottom of the waterway, where they may be buried and removed from the water system. Some pollutants do not break down or alter and so remain in the water system.

Anything that is flushed down a toilet, runs through a sink, or flows into a sewer drain from the street becomes sewage. Sewage is made up of 95% water. The remaining 5% is mostly human waste but also includes oil, toxic chemicals, fertilizers, pharmaceuticals (drugs), pesticides, and **pathogens** (disease-causing microscopic viruses, bacteria, and protozoans). The organic material is biodegradable, but the litter, pathogens, and synthetic (man made) chemicals are not.

Sewage may be treated before it runs into lakes and streams, but often it is not. In industrialized nations, most sewage goes through a sewage treatment plant; even so, it is not always cleansed. The sewage treatment systems of many large cities are now old and overextended. Storms cause wastewater to overflow, causing sewage to flood directly into streams and lakes. The available treatment regimens fail to remove some pollutants, such as parasite eggs, nutrients, and synthetic organic chemicals. Developing nations, on the other hand, often cannot afford to build sewage treatment plants in the first place. Worldwide, on average, 90% of wastewater enters inland waterways untreated. Large cities release hundreds of millions of tons of raw sewage into local waterways each year. Drinking or swimming in contaminated water results in hundreds of millions of cases of intestinal diseases worldwide annually.

Water that flows across roadways and rooftops, and over landfills and contaminated soil, often drains directly into streams or lakes. An acre of paved surface has 15 times more runoff than an acre of natural forest or meadow. Runoff from a city may be contaminated with oil, pollutants consisting of pesticides or fertilizers, chemicals from improperly maintained landfills, pathogens from pet waste, road salts, and heavy metals from mines and other sources. Polluted runoff is the greatest source of water quality problems in the United States. Nowadays, more American cities are diverting roadway runoff to sewage treatment plants. Still, some pollutants, specifically fertilizers and other chemical compounds, are not removed in the treatment plants and manage to enter surface waters.

AIR POLLUTION

Most medium and large cities around the Earth are contaminated with air pollutants because cities have large concentrations of fossil-fuel-burning engines and industrial plants. Sprawl increases air pollution because people are more likely to drive for longer distances and are less likely to have access to decent public transportation.

Air pollutants have a variety of ill effects: They raise global temperature, destroy natural atmospheric processes, and cause damage to the environment and human health. Air pollutants in cities come largely from fossil fuels, but they may have other sources. Air pollutants that are produced by the activities that take place in cities include the following:

⊕ Toxic gases, such as nitrogen dioxide (NO_2), sulfur dioxide (SO_2), and carbon monoxide (CO), which are released when fossil fuels are burned. NO_2 is a noxious, reddish-brown gas that contributes to the mucky russet color and odor of air in polluted cities. The concentration of nitrogen oxides in urban areas is 10 to 100 times greater than in rural areas. CO is a greenhouse gas and is toxic in confined spaces such as tunnels.

⊕ Nitrogen wastes from fossil fuels create nitrates in the atmosphere, which fall into the water and act as nutrients. Nitrogen from air pollution contributes to problems with eutrophication.

⊕ **Particulates** from burning fossil fuels and biomass create solid particles such as ash and soot.

⊕ Heavy metals, such as mercury and lead, come from burning fossil fuels and other materials.

⊕ **Ozone** is a secondary air pollutant that forms from fossil-fuel burning, especially in cars and trucks. This gas is the major component of **photochemical smog**, which forms by a chemical reaction between a primary pollutant, such as nitrogen or sulfur oxide, and a component of air, such as water vapor or hydrocarbons. Ozone pollution is worst on sunny summer days, when a white haze settles over the arid, car-dependent cities of southern California, southern Arizona, and Texas. This noxious, bad-smelling gas damages human lungs and poses serious harm to animals and plants. Ozone is also a greenhouse gas.

⊕ Sulfur and nitrogen oxides from fossil fuels form acids that fall as acid rain and create acid streams and lakes.

⊕ Ozone-destroying compounds, such as **chlorofluorocarbons** (CFCs) and other man-made chemicals from aerosols and other sources, damage the ozone layer in the upper atmosphere that protects the planet from the effects of the Sun's harmful ultraviolet radiation. (The ozone in the upper atmosphere is beneficial but in the lower atmosphere is a pollutant.)

⊕ Excess heat, which comes off engines, increases the temperature of cities. Man made surfaces, such as concrete and asphalt, also increase the city's temperatures by absorbing rather than reflecting the Sun's rays. Excess heat can also be considered a pollutant, and urban areas suffer from increased temperature and more variable weather as a result. This phenomenon is called the **urban heat island effect**.

⊕ Greenhouse gases come primarily from fossil fuel burning, which is increased by urbanization, particularly urban sprawl. One frightening scenario is projected for China: In 30 years, the urban population will increase by more than 750 million city dwellers. If each of these people uses transportation in the same way residents of the San Francisco Bay Area did in 1990, the amount of additional carbon released will exceed 1 billion tons (0.91 billion metric tons), about the same as the total amount released from all road transportation worldwide in 1998.

POLLUTION IN CITIES IN DEVELOPED AND DEVELOPING NATIONS

Each developed nation has a version of a Clean Air Act or Clean Water Act. Cities in these countries are cleaner in many ways than they were several decades ago. Technological solutions have reduced the major air pollutants and water pollutants in these nations. Yet, cities in developed countries still produce pollutants. Levels of photochemical smog have increased in the cities where it is prone to form. Greenhouse gases remain unregulated in many nations, including the United States, and are regulated only to a small extent in the European Union (EU) and a few other countries. Polluted runoff causes enormous problems in waterways near cities. Some chemicals and nutrients are unregulated and find their way into the water supply.

Far worse is the pollution in the expanding cities of the developing world. As these communities struggle to rise out of poverty, little attention is paid to the environmental degradation that accompanies economic development. In some nations, pollution has become an enormous side effect of a booming economy. In China, where 39% of the population is now urban, the economy is soaring, and pollution has increased by about 50% during the past decade. Sixteen of the

20 cities identified as having the greatest air pollution globally are in China. The nation's Ministry of Science and Technology says that air pollution kills 50,000 newborn babies and causes 400,000 premature deaths a year. Already, 70% of the country's lakes and rivers are unsuitable for human use, and the pollution is rapidly getting worse.

HEALTH EFFECTS OF CHANGES IN LAND USE

Urbanization also increases disease in both humans and in wild animals. As changing land use brings people and animals into closer contact, diseases pass more easily between them. In the mid-1990s, as many as one-third of the lions in Tanzania and Kenya died from canine distemper, spread to them by wild jackals and hyenas that, in turn, got the disease from village dogs. In that instance, a massive dog vaccination program has eliminated the problem and allowed the lion population to grow. (The lions, however, have other problems caused by the growth of human settlements, as the spread of villages near wildlife reserves leads the cats to hunt the villagers' domesticated animals. In turn, the villagers hunt the lions.)

Disease is an even greater problem for the great apes because they are so closely related to humans. When these animals are exposed to human diseases against which they have no immunity, such as flu and pneumonia, they usually die. The most frightening disease currently making its way through ape populations is Ebola, which causes uncontrollable bleeding in humans and apes. Ebola has a very high mortality rate and, over the past decade or so, has killed tens of thousands of the great apes in central Africa.

As humans come into greater contact with wildlife, the humans become exposed to more diseases. About 75% of human diseases have links to wildlife. When people move into deforested tropical regions, the malaria rates increase. Just as apes are susceptible to diseases carried by humans, humans, in turn, are susceptible to pathogens that are harbored by African apes and monkeys. For example, the introduction of HIV, the virus that causes AIDS, into humans has been traced to the consumption of chimpanzee meat.

WRAP-UP

Expanding cities have far-reaching environmental effects. Because of their high population density, cities produce vast quantities of pollution that affect the air, water, soil, climate, and even the upper atmospheric ozone layer. Most of the world's annual population increase of 75 million will take place in cities, primarily in the slums of the developing world. Whether these cities and the cities of the developed world will be clean and inhabitable depends greatly on how they grow and develop.

Sustainable Communities

This chapter discusses how, in the United States, some individual home builders, housing developments, and cities are working toward sustainability. Their main goal is to live without exhausting natural resources and to do this while being environmentally and economically stable. Achieving this goal is very difficult because so much of modern society is based on the automobile, which uses large amounts of fossil fuels; and centrally located supplies of food and other commodities are located at great distances from people's homes. A sustainable community of any size often gets its resources from surrounding communities. Still, whole cities, like Chicago, are attempting to become greener.

GREEN BUILDINGS

Several features can be built into a new house or other new building to make it more environmentally sound. Sometimes called green buildings, these structures are usually built in harmony with the natural environment. For instance, the house's placement, construction, and insulation can all be designed to take advantage of sunlight during the time of year when it is desirable and block it off when it is not. The features of a green building depend greatly on the climate of the area where the building is located: A house in a wintry location needs to be well insulated and be able to maximize solar input year round, while a desert dwelling needs to minimize the impact of the summer sun. Besides being more environmentally sound, these homes save the residents money by having lower operating costs.

A well-designed home can be constructed from natural materials such as straw bale, rammed earth, and adobe. The walls of straw bale homes are made from straw, an agricultural waste product, which is compressed into blocks and covered by stucco. Rammed earth is a mixture of sand, gravel, clay, and a stabilizer that is compressed and

Construction on a rammed earth house outside Phoenix, Arizona. The thick rammed earth walls provide insulation from the desert heat. *(James Elser)*

formed into the desired shape. Adobe is a mixture of sand, mud, straw, and other organic materials, such as animal dung, that is formed into bricks and dried in the Sun. All of these alternative building materials have good thermal mass: They heat up slowly during the day and lose heat gradually at night, thereby evening out daily temperature variations. In hot regions, where these materials are especially popular, the walls of the houses must be thick enough to keep cool during the day but thin enough to radiate heat during the night. Most of these green buildings have passive solar heating and may not need any additional heating and cooling. Homes can also be designed to collect rainwater for use in gardening, toilets, or other nondrinking purposes.

GREEN COMMUNITIES

In some locations, like-minded people band together to build a sustainable community. Such communities usually have environmentally sound housing as described above. The other features the community is likely to incorporate are:

⊕ Thoughtful land use: Residences are high density, with ample parks and other green spaces nearby. If additional land is available, it is kept pastoral or as natural habitat. The amenities that residents desire are centrally located and easily accessible. These might include recreational features such as a swimming pool, park, or gymnasium. (There is much less impact on the environment if a community has one large pool, rather than every house having its own smaller pool). In larger communities, there might be a community school or library.

⊕ "Green" transportation: The community is pedestrian friendly, with many residents walking to work, school, childcare, and shopping. Residents have easy access to public transportation. For residents who have cars, parking may be peripheral to living areas so that residents cannot drive to their homes. Besides keeping the community from being dominated by cars, this action is more pedestrian friendly, allowing people to interact with one another, thereby contributing to the sense of community.

⊕ Efficient water use: Rainwater may be collected for use in gardens or other activities, or it may be allowed to slip through cracks in patios and walkways so that it can filter into the soil. Rather than connecting to a sewage system, wastewater may be treated within the community. Some developments have built a wetlands system that treats and recycles all wastewater.

⊕ Alternative energy use: The community is likely to develop the sustainable energy source that is most suited to the local environment. Many communities use passive solar but may also harness active solar, geothermal, wind, or other energy types.

⊕ Sustainable food availability: Residents may be concerned about modern agricultural practices and may grow at least some of the community's food in community gardens. Some communities may encourage participation in a Community Supported Agriculture (CSA) plan.

GREEN CITIES

Many people now believe that the most environmentally sound way for large numbers of people to live close together is in well-designed "ecocities." These cities are beneficial because they concentrate the problems of human habitation to a confined area, thus making them easier to deal with. Ecocities have less urban sprawl, with a larger proportion of land that is free, or somewhat free, from human influence. With more people living in a smaller space, public transportation can be better developed, so less time is spent driving.

An important feature of ecocities is green high-rise buildings. The goal of Battery Park City, in lower Manhattan, New York City, is for all the buildings soon to be certified green by the United States Green Building Council (GBC). The GBC certification process has very stringent rules, and its buildings are models for other green buildings around the world. Green high-rise buildings incorporate the use of renewable materials, energy efficiency, water conservation, green rooftops, organic gardening, certified sustainably harvested wood, chemical-free paint and other materials, well-filtered air, construction waste recycling, and "gray water" recycling (which involves reusing laundry or shower water for irrigation). Preexisting buildings in Battery Park City are being retrofitted to incorporate some of these features. Developers are increasingly attracted to constructing green buildings as they learn that people will pay more to live in them.

In some cases, entire cities are attempting to be environmentally sensitive. Chicago, Illinois, has been going green since Richard M. Daley became mayor in 1989. Chicago's new buildings are currently the most environmentally sensitive under construction in the United States. The city helps out by granting building permits more quickly to those who are planning green buildings than to those who are not. The city is also encouraging everyone to conserve resources, save energy, generate clean and renewable energy, reduce storm-water runoff, restore wetlands, and repair neighborhoods and parks. Since 1989, approximately 500,000 trees have been planted, all of them fertilized with mulch. Gardens and green spaces have been constructed and expanded, mostly on rooftops. The largest rooftop garden is Millennium Park, which sits above an underground parking lot. The 24.5-acre (9.92-hectare) park contains lawn, wild-grass prairie, gardens, and sculpture.

SMART GROWTH

One answer that ecocities have for the problem of urban sprawl is the principle of "smart growth." This philosophy has been adopted by a few communities in the United States, Canada, and elsewhere.

Cities that have embraced smart growth have zoning laws that restrict development to specific areas, minimize the amount of space devoted to parking, and require the development of parks and other amenities. The purpose of smart growth is to keep the people living in higher-density city centers while protecting the rural and natural landscapes on the outside. Cities embracing smart growth have densely settled interiors with mixed activities to encourage mass transit, bicycling, and walking. Restricting growth from moving outward encourages the development of abandoned or rundown industrial or urban areas, which is one way to keep city centers vital.

Residents of smart growth communities see many advantages. Mixed-use development allows people to live, shop, and work in the same neighborhood. Because people are less reliant on cars, they are more visible in their communities and are more likely to know their neighbors. Fewer cars also means less pollution; therefore, these cities are often cleaner. Because the city center is valued, there is a great emphasis on historic preservation. Growth boundaries cause the land within the urban area to become more valuable; therefore, parking lots and other low-use spaces are minimized. Parks and green spaces are often an important part of these communities.

In 1973, each community in Oregon set urban growth boundaries. Since then, Portland, the state's largest city, has experienced several changes. Between 1970 and 2000, the city's population grew by 400,000, and the city's area grew by 86 square miles (222 sq. km). Growth boundaries resulted in an increase in population density from 2,937 per square mile (1,134 per sq. km) in 1970 to 3,340 per square mile (1,290 per sq. km) in 2000, although the city still has a lower population density than the much larger cities New York or Los Angeles. To encourage walking, the city has compact blocks and narrow streets. Portland has a better-developed public transportation system and less traffic than other cities of its size. However, while these features fit with the smart growth model, the city has not regarded the urban growth boundaries as immutable: In 2004, Portland expanded beyond the boundary set for 2040.

Critics of smart growth say that restrictions to development cause housing prices to increase, sometimes to the point of making a detached house difficult for families with average incomes to afford. Even so, housing prices in Oregon are lower than in Washington State to the north and California to the south. Some people say that cities are unsafe and dirty, and people are better off in the suburbs. But Jane Jacobs, a "housewife" whose very influential 1961 book *The Death and Life of Great American Cities* changed the way people looked at cities, said that these things are only true when cities are empty. Cities are safe when they are crowded with people walking down the street and sitting on their stoops on a warm summer's evening. Cities thrive when they have mixed uses, when people are able to converge on parks and cultural events, and when they are proud of their city and work to preserve its character.

In her 2004 book, *Dark Age Ahead*, Jacobs was somewhat optimistic even though many communities seem to encourage sprawl. "At a given time it is hard to tell whether forces of cultural life or death are in the ascendancy. Is suburban sprawl, with its murders of communities and wastes of land, time, and energy, a sign of decay? Or is rising interest in means of overcoming sprawl a sign of vigor and adaptability in North American culture? Arguably, either could turn out to be true."

WRAP-UP

Great advances are being made in the research and development of more sustainable ways to live. Techniques are being developed for building greener homes and more sustainable communities. Some cities and smaller communities are adopting smart growth practices to encourage sensible development. By placing boundaries on urban growth, the cities with compact growth boundaries increase the value of inner city land, which eliminates abandoned lots and other useless landscapes and fills them with houses and workplaces. Dense inner-city development helps to protect rural and wild lands outside the city. However, despite the advantages of developing greener communities, most development does not yet adhere to sustainable growth.

PART SIX

WASTE DISPOSAL

Solid Waste Disposal

Human activities generate large amounts of wastes as gases, liquids, and solids. Gaseous and liquid wastes, and their role in air and water pollution, were discussed in previous chapters throughout this book. This chapter describes in further detail how solid wastes are often dumped on, or buried under, the land. In developed nations, where land is available, the trash is likely to wind up in a landfill. Where land is at a premium, as in Japan, trash is more likely to be incinerated. This chapter focuses on the wastes that are generated by homes and businesses, including the expanding problem of electronic waste. Solid wastes are best dealt with by not creating them in the first place or by reusing materials, as is suggested by the slogan "reduce, reuse, and recycle."

LANDFILLS

What happens to solid waste after it is collected by a garbage truck from the trash can in front of a suburban home? Most of the time, it is delivered by garbage trucks, which compact the waste during the journey, to a landfill. Ordinarily, these landfills are constructed in low-lying areas or holes in the ground, such as quarries. After the garbage is dumped into the pit, large, spike-wheeled vehicles drive over it to compact it further. The waste must be compacted so that it cannot be blown away by wind or become easily infested with rats. Environmentally sound landfills are lined with clay or plastic to keep the toxic fluids that ooze out of the refuse from permeating the underlying rock and reaching the groundwater aquifer. The best landfills combust the gases generated by decomposition—such as methane and carbon dioxide—to generate power. In others, the gases, which are greenhouse gases, are burned off to keep them from reaching the atmosphere. But even the best land-fills have a problem that is common to all: They are located far from where the waste is first generated because no one wants a landfill in the neighborhood. Because of this, transporting the refuse uses fossil fuels and creates air pollution. The worst landfills are those that are old or poorly managed: They are rat-infested, polluted, spread bad smells, and contribute to global warming.

Eighty percent of trash in the United States ends up in a landfill. Perhaps the country's best-known landfill is the Fresh Kills Landfill on Staten Island, New York. The landfill, formerly the world's largest, was the main waste-dumping site for New York City from 1948 to 2001. (After the terrorist attacks on the World Trade Center on September 11, 2001, the landfill was reopened to receive debris from the twin towers and nearby buildings. Most of that debris was processed and sold for scrap.)

Fresh Kills is currently undergoing a transformation. The site's proximity to New York City makes it some of the world's most valuable land. Using state-of-the-art reclamation techniques, the city plans to return the 2,200 acre site (8.9 sq. km), nearly three times the size of Central Park, to wetlands, open waterways, and lowland areas. When complete, the site will also be a location for recreation, public art, and sports facilities. Construction of the park is expected to begin in late 2007 and take 30 years.

As materials that were once abundant become scarce, landfills may someday become valuable mining sites. In some developing nations, poor people are already sifting through newly arrived trash looking for metals and other valuable objects that they can sell for scrap.

INCINERATION

Another way to dispose of trash is by burning. In land-scarce Japan, 80% of trash is incinerated. Incineration was once popular in the United States, but problems with air quality caused limits to be imposed on the number of locations, types of trash, and times of the year during which it could be burned. (However, medical and other potentially hazardous wastes are still incinerated for safety reasons.) When trash is incinerated, toxic gas and ash pollutes the air and, eventually, the downwind water supply.

Although modern, well-run incinerators keep exhaust gases from entering the atmosphere, the **dioxins** they produce have become a problem in recent years. Dioxins are toxic chemicals that have been shown to be hazardous to animals and possibly humans. Besides emitting pollutants, incineration so thoroughly destroys the waste and all that went into producing it, that remnants can never be mined for useful materials.

Some older incinerators do produce a small amount of useful material or energy. The ash from incinerators can be manufactured into lye and other chemicals, or it can be used in cement furnaces. The energy from the burning trash can also produce electricity, although this process is inefficient and produces only a little usable energy. Modern incinerators are more efficient than older incinerators at producing usable materials. The incineration of waste material in a sealed vessel under high temperature and pressure is a more efficient process for recovering usable energy. In pyrolysis, the waste converts to solid that can be refined to produce products such as activated carbon, liquid oil, and gas that can be burned for energy or refined into other products. In gasification, the waste converts into a synthetic gas made of carbon monoxide and hydrogen that is burned to produce electricity and steam.

THE MOUNTING PROBLEM OF ELECTRONIC WASTE

The fastest growing problem in waste management is electronic waste. "E-waste," as it is called, consists of any electrical appliance that is no longer useful: large and small household appliances, electronic toys and recreational equipment, and entertainment devices such as TVs and portable CD players.

The sheer amount of electronic trash is enormous. Each year, 20 to 50 million tons (18 to 45 million metric tons) of electronics are discarded: If they were placed in railroad containers, the train would circle the globe. The Environmental Protection Agency (EPA) estimates that Americans discard 2 million tons (1.8 million metric tons) of electronics each year, including 63 million computers.

Computers and mobile phones make up the largest source of e-waste: Globally, nearly 200 million new computers and 700 million mobile phones are sold every year. Many people want to buy the latest gadgets, which makes electronics obsolete at ever-increasing speeds. For instance, a computer has a lifespan of three to five years, while a mobile phone has only two. While much of this consumption takes place in developed nations, rapid growth in electronics use is occurring in the world's briskly expanding economies, including China and India.

But the waste amounts are only part of the problem. Most electronics contain significant amounts of toxic materials, including the heavy metals lead, zinc, chromium, mercury, cadmium, and more than 30 other chemical compounds. A computer may be as much as 6% lead by weight. The computer circuit boards and the glass surrounding the cathode ray tubes (CRTs) found in monitors and televisions are especially riddled with lead and other heavy metals. The lead intake leads to nervous system, brain, and blood disorders, especially in children.

E-waste can be disposed of safely by reuse or recycling. Old computers and other electronics can be reused—passed to others who do not need or cannot afford the latest models. However, electronics recycling is very difficult because the machines are complex mixtures of materials. In recycling, the equipment is first dismantled (usually by hand). Following that, high-tech machinery separates and processes the metals and plastics. While the metals are valuable and useful, the plastics are commonly not worth the effort it takes to process them because most contain flame retardants that cannot be easily recycled.

Because recycling is difficult, a lot of e-waste is treated like other trash. More than two million tons of electronics end up in landfills in the United States each year. According to federal law, it is legal to dump up to 220 pounds (100 kg) of e-waste into a landfill each month, including CRTs and circuit boards. Some states have their own, more stringent, e-waste laws: For example, they may forbid the dumping of CRTs in landfills. In California, buyers of new monitors and televisions must pay a fee to cover recycling costs.

Different nations deal with e-waste differently. The European Union (EU), South Korea, Japan, and Taiwan, where land is especially valuable, require recycling of most electronics. The European nations banned dumping e-waste in landfills in the 1990s, giving rise to a processing industry. European electronics manufacturers are required to take back their products and distribute them to legitimate recyclers. In the United States, many electronics manufacturers oppose instituting similar take-back laws, although some do so voluntarily. One company that does recycle its e-waste is Hewlett-Packard, which processes 18 million pounds (8 million kg) of electronic trash a year. This "ore" supplies about 8 to 10 ounces (220 to 280 grams) per ton of precious metals such as gold, silver, and palladium, as well as other substances.

However, many "recyclers" in the United States, Europe, and Japan ship their e-waste to developing nations, such as China and India. About 80% of the computers, mobile phones, and TVs collected for recycling in the United States wind up overseas. These recyclers exploit the cheap labor, corruption, and lax environmental laws of many of these nations. Once the shipment arrives, the electronics may be transported to rural areas out of the sight of regulators. The rural workers break the products apart, burn the plastic to free the metals, and put the gold-bearing materials in an acid bath to free the gold.

While this process provides an extremely valuable supply of scrap metal for these developing nations, it is a hazard to workers' health and to the environment. Ordinarily, the workers have no protection

A market scavenger boy in an electronics waste dump in Lagos, Nigeria. *(Basel Action Network)*

and suffer direct exposure to toxic materials. The wastes are dumped into streams, burned, or placed in unlined dumps. In Guiyu, China, e-waste recyclers and their children live and work in the same area. The region's water supply has lead concentrations 400 to 600 times the international safety standards and has been undrinkable since the mid-1990s. The heavy metals found in the waste accumulate in the blood and act as endocrine disruptors, while the plastic waste breaks down or is burned to form agents that may cause cancer. As much as 75% of the material is unusable and remains in the region as toxic trash.

The Basel Convention of the United Nations Environment Programme (UNEP) prohibits the export of hazardous waste from developed to developing nations, although electronics are exempted from this rule if they are exported for recycling. The convention has been ratified by all industrialized nations except the United States, which is currently looking at the Basel Convention and other proposed laws to try to find a unified policy for dealing with e-waste.

Companies are also beginning to reduce the amount of toxic material they use when manufacturing computers. For example, they are now reducing the amount of lead they use in the glass tubes of CRTs (the lead protects the computer and television users from the X-rays emitted by the CRT) and replacing it with other metal alloys (which are more expensive and harder to work with). They are also replacing the CRTs with liquid-crystal displays.

Efforts to decrease the toxicity of e-waste are partly the result of restrictions imposed by members of the EU, which, since July 2006, have been severely restricting the use of the most hazardous materials used in electronic manufacture. Besides lead, restrictions are in place for mercury, cadmium, a form of chromium that is a known carcinogen, and two flame retardants (PBB and PBDE) that can harm the human endocrine and skeletal systems. While these restrictions only apply to products sold in the EU at this time, manufacturers who sell the same products globally are working to meet these restrictions on a worldwide basis.

A few companies are doing research into using plant materials instead of fossil fuels to create plastics for use in electronics, especially cell phones. So far, these materials have proved to be too brittle and heat sensitive.

REDUCE, REUSE, RECYCLE

Waste management is a large problem for some metropolitan areas, especially where there is little land for landfills and where incineration would mean polluting the air for millions of people. One important aspect of waste management, and one that will become more crucial in the future, is to reduce the amount of waste that is generated. This can be done in two ways: (1) reducing consumption, which has other positive environmental effects, such as less energy use and less pollution;

and (2) reducing the amount of packaging, which reduces the waste, energy, and pollution that result from manufacturing and disposing of the packaging.

Reusing material can mean cleaning and refilling individual containers, such as those used for food or beverages. This can be done on an individual level, such as by storing leftovers in an old yogurt carton, or it can be done on a larger scale within a community. For example, in some locations, soda bottles come with a refundable deposit to be paid when they are returned. Each bottle is then cleaned, refilled, and sold again. In many European countries, refillable bottles are the norm, as they are in developing nations such as India, where the cost of new materials is very high. In the United States, though, this system passed out of favor a few decades ago; in most states, bottles and cans are more likely to be recycled.

Recycling is the breakdown of a waste material so that it can be remade into a new product: for example, the recycling of used plastic bottles into new plastic bottles or other plastic materials. Most items that are composed of a single type of material can be recycled. Commonly recycled materials include glass, paper, aluminum, and steel. Preconsumer waste (material used in manufacturing) or postconsumer waste (materials that have been used by consumers) can be recycled.

But recycling is not a cure-all for the waste problem. While recycling certainly reduces waste and the consumption of new materials, it also consumes a great deal more energy than does reuse. Some material is lost every time an item is recycled, so recycling the same material cannot take place indefinitely. Also, recycled materials may not be of the same quality. For example, recycled paper has shorter fibers than high-grade paper. And, if contamination occurs, the recycled materials cannot be made into products such as food containers.

Recycling materials has a lesser impact on the environment than creating objects from virgin materials, however. Recycling usually uses less energy, water, and other resources. For example, producing aluminum from bauxite requires 5 times as much material as collecting the metal from aluminum cans and requires 20 times the energy. For these reasons, some cities, such as New York and Seattle, impose fines on people who throw away recyclable material. Yet, in many other instances, the cost of collecting, sorting, and processing the waste means that recycled materials are often more expensive than virgin materials.

To encourage recycling, several states have reintroduced the policy of paying a refund on beverage bottles. Oregon was the first state to pass a bottle bill whereby each bottle and can in the state has a 5-cent deposit. This system's 90% return rate has reduced waste and conserved resources, such as aluminum. (States without bottle bills average 28% return on containers). In some states, these deposits are used to fund more widespread recycling efforts.

WRAP-UP

Because human activities generate so much trash, waste disposal is an extremely important land-use issue. Whether the waste is household trash or electronic waste, it must be disposed of properly. Waste managers must take precautions to isolate it from atmospheric, aquatic, and biological systems for as long as necessary. Waste disposal issues will become more important as populations continue to grow, available land area continues to shrink, and people in the developed and developing world continue to increase their consumption of material goods. The best way to deal with trash is to stop making it by reducing consumption, reusing products, and recycling materials that cannot be reused.

Nuclear Waste Disposal

This chapter discusses high-level nuclear waste, a waste disposal problem unlike any other because the material remains hazardous for more than 10,000 years. Every nation with nuclear power plants has plans for storing these wastes safely. In the United States, the Yucca Mountain Repository in Nevada has been studied for decades for its suitability as a high-level nuclear waste disposal site.

NUCLEAR WASTE DISPOSAL

Nuclear waste contains radioactive chemical elements that are no longer useful. Radioactive wastes are the result of scientific, medical, military, and industrial activities, such as medical tests, nuclear power generation, and nuclear bomb development programs.

A radioactive substance is only hazardous as long as it is radioactive: Once it has decayed, it is no more harmful than any other type of matter. Low-level radioactive wastes, such as most medical wastes, have short half-lives. They must be kept isolated for a matter of days

Radioactivity

Some isotopes have nuclei that are naturally unstable. To achieve stability, these nuclei gain or emit a particle, a process called **radioactive decay**. The addition or loss of a particle changes the number of protons in the nucleus, and, thus, a new element is formed. For example, if a proton in a potassium-40 ion is hit with a negatively charged beta particle, that proton will become a neutron. This changes the number of protons in the nucleus to 18 and the number of neutrons to 22, so the potassium-40 becomes argon-40. Radioactive isotopes can also be created artificially by bombarding stable nuclei with particles in an accelerator. An enormous amount of heat is given off during radioactive decay.

In a batch of radioactive material, the transformation of one element (the parent) into another (the daughter) by radioactive decay occurs gradually. Although it is impossible to know when a single radioactive nucleus will decay, the rate at which a group of nuclei decays is constant and known for each radioactive element. The amount of time necessary for half of the nuclei of the unstable parent isotope to convert to the stable daughter isotope is called the **half-life** of the isotope. The half-life of a radioactive

(continues)

Half-Lives of Some Radioactive Isotopes

PARENT ISOTOPE	DAUGHTER ISOTOPE	HALF LIFE
Platinum-158	Osmium-164	0.002 seconds
Iodine-131	Xenon-131	8.05 days
Carbon-14	Nitrogen-14	5,730 years
Neptunium-237*	Protactinium-233	2,144,000 years
Potassium-40	Argon-40	1,310,000,000 years
Uranium-238	Lead-206	4,510,000,000 years

This isotope is formed in nuclear reactors.

(continues)

isotope may range from a fraction of a second to billions of years. A radioactive daughter may itself be unstable and undergo radioactive decay. In that case, the result is a decay series with a string of daughter isotopes until the final stable daughter isotope is produced. One example is uranium-238, which has lead-206 as its final daughter.

Examples of various half-lives are seen in the table on page 165.

or years until they have decayed enough that they can be safely placed in an ordinary landfill. High-level radioactive wastes have extremely long half-lives and are hazardous for enormous periods of time. They must be kept isolated from living creatures for millennia until they have mostly decayed.

Much of the existing high-level radioactive waste is contained in spent fuel rods from nuclear reactors. A commercial nuclear reactor contains about 50,000 fuel rods. Each of these fuel rods contains pellets of radioactive uranium. One of these hand-sized uranium pellets contains the same amount of energy as one ton (.91 metric tons) of coal.

After three or four years, the fuel rods in these reactors are no longer efficient and so must be discarded. When the rods are first removed from the reactor, they are extremely hot and radioactive. Initially, they are stored for at least one year in a spent fuel pool, a deep pit filled with water that cools the rods while their short-lived isotopes undergo radioactive decay. Next, the rods are processed for reuse or are moved to dry cask storage, where they are placed in steel containers surrounded by a chemically inert gas to keep them from sending radioactivity into their surrounding environment.

Currently, high-level nuclear waste is stored at 126 sites around the United States, mostly near the reactors where it was first generated. Experts estimate that these storage facilities will be completely filled by 2014. While dry cask storage may be safe temporarily (and there is some controversy surrounding this assumption), the casks will certainly not withstand tens of thousands of years of rain, wind, geological activity, and social changes without leaking high-level radioactive waste into the environment. By the time the currently available dry cask storage facilities are filled, the government hopes that the nuclear waste will be moved for permanent storage to the Yucca Mountain Repository, Nevada.

YUCCA MOUNTAIN REPOSITORY

The high-level radioactive waste destined for long-term storage has some important characteristics: It is solid (the only safe way it can be stored), nonexplosive (even if a bomb went off within it), and nonflammable.

However, its most significant characteristic is that it will be dangerously radioactive for more than 10,000 years. Due to this incredibly long time period, scientists from around the world have concluded that the best place for high-level nuclear waste storage is in a stable geological formation.

The United States is currently working toward developing a nuclear waste repository in the remote desert at Yucca Mountain, Nevada. The Yucca Mountain Repository is intended to be the final resting place for spent nuclear fuel from power plants and high-level radioactive waste defense projects from around the country. Yucca Mountain was chosen in 1987 from nine locations in six states that had undergone preliminary study. Since that time, hundreds of scientists have analyzed all aspects of the environment of Yucca Mountain, so much that a white paper issued by the U.S. Senate Committee on Environment and Public Works in March 2006 was entitled "Yucca Mountain: The Most Studied Real Estate on the Planet." More than $7 billion has been spent on the project so far. In 2002, President George W. Bush decided to push for the next step and authorized the preparation of an application for the building of the repository to be submitted to the Nuclear Regulatory Commission.

The proposed repository is an area of 1,150 acres (4.7 sq. km), 1,000 feet (300 m) below the ground surface and 1,000 feet (300 m) above the groundwater aquifer. Two types of natural phenomena could breach the site and spread radioactivity: water and geological activity such as earthquakes and volcanic eruptions. These and other concerns—and other advantages and disadvantages of the Yucca Mountain site—are looked at in the list that follows.

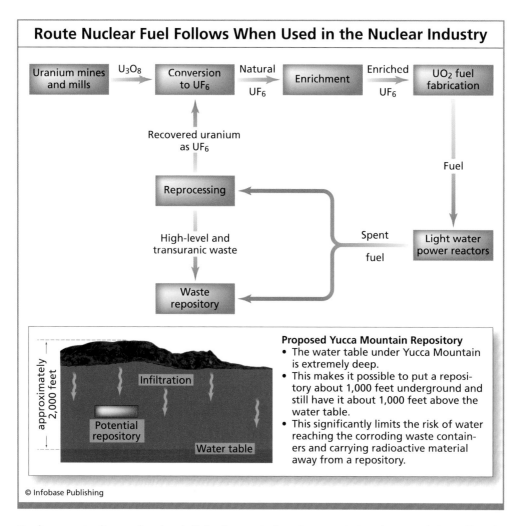

Route Nuclear Fuel Follows When Used in the Nuclear Industry

© Infobase Publishing

Nuclear waste disposal on land. Safe disposal of nuclear waste has been an international concern for many decades. Yucca Mountain is the U.S. government's potential geologic repository designed to store approximately 70,000 tons of spent nuclear fuel and high-level radioactive waste.

A 1.7-mile (2.7 km) long tunnel used for scientific studies in the potential high-level nuclear waste repository at Yucca Mountain, Nevada.
(U.S. Department of Energy)

- Arid climate: This part of Nevada gets less than 7.5 inches (19 cm) of rainfall a year, nearly all of which evaporates or runs off the mountain. Only about 5% of rainfall reaches the depth of the repository. Opponents of the site say that in the geologic past, the region received much more rain, and the water table was higher, so no one can predict what the climate will be like in 10,000 years. In response, proponents of the site say that even if there is more rain, seepage is slow enough that the water will not be radioactive by the time it reaches the water table. To further guard against the intrusion of water, the radioactive waste will be sealed in extremely durable metal packages that will be placed in deep underground tunnels and covered with corrosion-resistant metal.

- Remoteness: The repository is an area of 230 square miles (596 sq. km) lying within the Nevada test site, which covers an area of 1,375 square miles (3,561 sq. km) of already highly restricted land. Surrounding the test site are 5,470 square miles (14,200 square km) of public lands that are either designated as wildlife refuges or as U.S. Air Force ranges with restricted air space above and well-established high security on the ground. The nearest population center is 15 miles (24 km) away in the Amargosa Valley. The site is also 100 miles (160 km) northwest of Las Vegas. Opponents of the site say that land use patterns are likely to change over the next 10 millennia.

⊕ Geology: Yucca Mountain is a ridge composed of rock layers that were laid down in volcanic eruptions between 11 and 14 million years ago. The dominant rock type is tuff, an ash that has been welded by extremely high heat. While volcanic activity appears to have ceased in the area, earthquakes are extremely common. Most of these quakes are tiny, but a magnitude 4.4 quake shook the area in 2002, and a 5.6 occurred in 1992, with both their epicenters located approximately 12 miles (20 km) southeast of the potential waste repository. Nonetheless, precariously perched boulders in some of the area's rock formations indicate that there has not been any significant ground movement at the site in thousands of years.

⊕ Deep aquifer: The groundwater aquifer lies deep beneath the proposed repository. Cracks in the rock appear to extend down to the water table, allowing a route for radioactive waste to travel once the containers have been breached (as they surely will be over such an enormous length of time). Proponents of the site say that the waste would likely be safe by the time it traveled through so much rock down to the water table. Opponents think that contaminated water will eventually work its way down into the aquifer.

⊕ Closed water basin: Yucca Mountain is in a basin, surrounded by higher land. The region is so arid that there is only minimal surface water flow, and that occurs only after a storm. Groundwater remains within the basin and does not flow to the surface. The groundwater does not reach population centers such as Las Vegas.

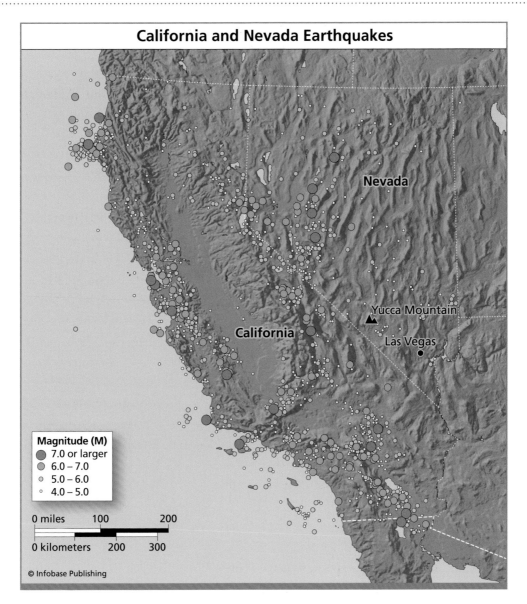

Earthquakes of California and Nevada from 1769 to 2005. The Yucca Mountain Nuclear Waste Repository will be located on the ridge. While the seismic activity here is not as great as in other parts of Nevada, there have been significant earthquakes in the past 250 years.

Government officials hope that the repository will open between 2010 and 2017. Once open, the site will accept waste for between 50 and 300 years. When the site is full, the repository will be permanently sealed.

In 1987, when Yucca Mountain was chosen as the only site to be pursued, Congress stated that if the site was later found to be unsuitable, studies would stop immediately, the landscape would be restored to its natural state, and a new direction would be found. Although there have been many objections, none have caused the federal government to reconsider proceeding with developing the site. The strongest objections have come from Nevada residents who oppose the facility for issues of safety and fairness (Nevada does not even have a nuclear power plant). Nevada's governor filed an official objection to proceeding with plans in 2002, but the objection was overruled by Congress.

If Yucca Mountain or any other centrally located site is opened for long-term radioactive waste storage, the waste will be shipped in by rail. Many people are concerned that there may be accidents or terrorist activities that could be disastrous for the millions of people who live in the areas through which the waste will be transported. Yet, nuclear waste is routinely shipped in Europe and Asia, and there have been few safety issues.

After much study, the conclusion of the Senate Committee on Environment and Public Works in 2006 was to move forward without further delay. Whether the Yucca Mountain Repository ever opens remains to be seen. If it does not, much work will need to be done to find another site that is more suitable.

WRAP-UP

Critics and supporters debate the pluses and minuses of nuclear power, with both sides making many good points. In the absence of an accident, nuclear energy is nonpolluting and environmentally safe, at least when compared with fossil fuels. While there is always the possibility of an accident, new plants can be designed to be much safer than they were several decades ago. But high-level nuclear waste disposal is a sticking point. Human beings were very different 10,000 years ago (there is no record of any Neolithic human having used a metal tool) and likely will be very different 10,000 years from now. A new study suggesting that Yucca Mountain can keep wastes safe for 1,000,000 years represents 25,000 human generations. To suggest that nuclear wastes can be disposed of carefully and kept safely over such tremendous periods of time seems to many critics to be folly.

Conclusion

People are rapidly changing the land from natural to human landscapes. Already, about half of the land has been altered for human uses; and much more of it will undergo changes in the coming decades, as population grows and the desire for consumer goods grows with it, particularly among people living in the developing nations. In their search for resources, people convert vast expanses of natural terrain to landscapes that better meet their needs: forests into tree farms, and wilderness to agricultural land. Even farmland is paved over to make way for urban environments. Areas where mineral and energy resources are discovered are mined. All of these activities produce waste products: pollutants that enter the air and water, and waste materials that must be disposed of somewhere. One type of waste—high-level nuclear waste—will remain hazardous for unfathomably long periods of time.

Some of the points that were made about land use in this volume are summarized here:

⊕ Vast amounts of forest are being logged wholly or selectively, damaging the forests that remain. Forests are being replaced by tree plantations, farms, or ranches, which do not resemble healthy forest ecosystems. Deforested land is highly prone to erosion.

⊕ The abuse of agricultural lands results in soil degradation and erosion. Farmers who work on these deficient soils use machinery, chemical fertilizers, pesticides, and other environmentally destructive practices to stay in business. Traditional farmers, unable to compete in this new environment, are driven from their land and usually end up in a city.

⊕ Extremely valuable farmland is being paved over for houses, businesses, and roadways. These urban environments could instead be built on land that is less suitable for farming.

⊕ Urban areas expand as more people move to the city and as residents demand larger homes and lots. Single-family homes now house fewer people; thus, more houses are needed. One result is bloated cities with populations that depend on cars for transportation.

⊕ Mining companies take the resources they want and leave behind a heavily altered and polluted landscape. The cost for cleaning this mess often falls to taxpayers or a cleanup fund that is financed by other companies. In developing nations, cleanup is often disregarded altogether.

⊕ The day-to-day wastes generated in cities in developed nations are usually disposed of properly. However, more people creating more waste means that waste must be carted farther into rural and wild lands. At this time, the growing amount of electronic waste is dealt with poorly, although companies and nations are beginning to grapple with this enormous problem.

⊕ In the rush to generate nuclear power, which is clean and inexpensive, no one has solved the problem of what to do with long-term radioactive waste.

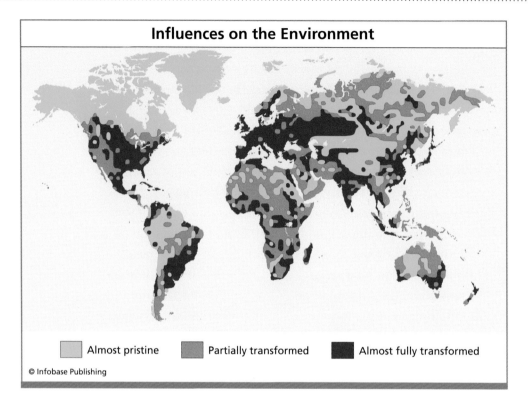

Human transformation of the land. While a considerable proportion of the world's land mass can be classified as "almost pristine," relatively little land has completely escaped human activity. Human-induced climate change and the effects of pesticides and other chemicals are expected to profoundly change those parts of the world that have escaped deliberate transformation.

When it comes to land use, it seems as if there is no one in charge. No one is commanding that we use the land efficiently and well. No one is making sure that the choices being made today are minimally damaging to future generations—that is, that the choices being made are based on the idea of sustainable use. Perhaps there is no better illustration of this problem than the loss of prime farmland to urbanization, as is happening in California's Central Valley. This area contains exceptionally fertile soil, easily accessible irrigation, and favorable weather—the best farmland in the world. Yet it is under serious pressure from developers who could instead build housing in another location, such as the nearby foothills of the Sierra Nevada Mountains, where the rocky hillsides make less suitable farmland.

There are many other problems with the large-scale conversion of natural landscapes to human landscapes. Forests and other ecosystems have evolved over millions of years as a harmonious structure. Tree farms and croplands are not designed to obey the laws of nature; they are designed to generate profit. These systems are therefore extremely vulnerable to such changing conditions as disease, changing climate, invasive species, pollution, and other problems, many of which are brought about by humans. For example, if a new pest species with a taste for corn and a resistance to modern pesticides entered the midwestern United States, it could multiply rapidly and decimate the crop. As a result, the food supply would decrease, and people could go hungry.

Already, human influences have caused fires to become much more damaging than they were in the geologic past. The past 100 years of fire suppression has resulted in the buildup of leaves and other waste on the forest floor that causes fires to burn hotter and higher on the trees than fires have burned in the past. Drier conditions and the spread of insect pests have made the forests even more vulnerable.

While nuclear power is attractive at this time, because it is non-polluting and does not produce greenhouse gases, generating nuclear wastes that must be kept isolated from the environment for more than 10,000 years may not be a good idea. Is it prudent to think that the people of the far distant future will be willing and able to care for the wastes generated by people today? A more sensible approach might be to develop sustainable energy sources that are suitable for a given location: for example, solar power for arid and semiarid regions, wind energy for places with suitable wind levels, and geothermal power for locations where hot rock lies close to the surface, among other alternatives.

Although no one seems to be in charge of land use issues on a national or international level, individuals and communities are beginning to make changes on a local level: by making small changes in their habits, consuming less, or recycling more. Some design green houses, which may derive their energy from the Sun, obtain most of their water from rain, recycle wastewater through a constructed wetland, and be built of natural, locally derived materials. Green cities are defined by green buildings, ample parks and green spaces, good public transportation, and growth boundaries.

Individuals and communities are turning more toward sustainable agriculture. In recent years, there has been an explosion of interest in producing food that is healthy for individuals and for the environment and selling it locally. Supporting local farmers helps them keep their farms economically viable and keeps them from selling them to make room for encroaching subdivisions. Supporting local farms allows a region to maintain its rural identity.

When it comes to land use, individuals can vote with their pocketbooks, perhaps more than in any other realm. There are many things an individual can do, particularly regarding agriculture—after all, people need to eat every day. Here are a few things that an individual can do:

- Buy locally grown, organic foods. Buying locally reduces energy consumption and pollution by eliminating the need for lengthy food transportation. Buying organic keeps the environment free of pesticides, excess nutrients, and pharmaceuticals that can cause health problems for wildlife and humans. To buy local food, search out a farmer's market, food co-op, or Community Supported Agriculture (CSA) system.
- Grow your own produce, adhering to the principles of organic farming.
- Be especially careful about buying meat because it takes large amounts of energy to produce. Organic, locally grown meats are the best option.
- Avoid products with a large amount of packaging. These materials waste resources in their manufacture and are of little use. A plastic water bottle performs a very minor job, yet it will survive intact in a landfill for hundreds of years

or, if recycled, will require using energy to clean and transform it for reuse.

⊕ Look into using alternative energy—solar, wind, geothermal, or biomass—for home or transportation.

⊕ Minimize the use of wood products. Conserve paper. When buying furniture, be sure it is certified as being produced sustainably.

⊕ Use renewable resources whenever possible. Wood and some types of energy are renewable.

⊕ Monitor consumption. When choosing a living space or a car, go for only what is needed. A small car can get people where they want to go just as well as a big one.

⊕ When traveling, try ecotourism. Sustainable travel ensures that the land will be preserved for future tourists and future residents of the region.

⊕ Much mining is done without regard to the future of the people who live in the region, particularly in those countries where international corporations extract the resources and leave behind damaged land and dangerous levels of pollution. Try to avoid using resources that were extracted in this way, particularly gold. A movement to encourage jewelers to buy gold from mining operations that do not use cyanide is beginning and can be a resource for information when jewelry shopping.

This is where changes begin: with one person and one family. A knowledgeable person can make choices that can impact how society operates: For example, by supporting sustainable agriculture, more farmers will be able to practice environmentally sound methods, and more rural landscapes will survive.

As with so many issues, knowledge allows people to make important political decisions. In the case of protecting the geosphere, people can encourage their elected politicians to support sustainable land use. Aware citizens will vote for those politicians who see beyond the short-term economic gain to the long-term future of the planet. And they will work to elect those who support the adoption of sustainable practices in the United States and internationally.

Young people will play a major role in implementing change by educating themselves on the needs of the world and its environment, and bringing along their hope and enthusiasm. The path the world is on can be turned, incrementally and completely, with knowledge, dedication, and determination.

Glossary

acid   A substance that releases hydrogen ions in solution; acidic solutions have numbers below 7 on the pH scale.

acid mine drainage   The flow of acid from a mine site, usually after the site has been abandoned; water draining the site becomes acidic as it flows through sulfide mineral–containing rock waste.

acid rain   Rainfall with a pH of less than 5.0. Acid rain is a type of acid precipitation, which includes acid fog and acid snow.

adaptation   A structure or behavior alteration that is inheritable; that is, able to be passed from one generation to the next.

aerobic   Word used to describe an environment containing oxygen or an organism that breathes oxygen.

air pollution   Contamination of the air by particulates and toxic gases in concentrations that can endanger human and environmental health. Also known as smog.

alien species   Organisms that are introduced by human activities into a location where they are not native; also called invasive species.

alkaline   Word used to describe a solution in which hydroxyl ion is present in excess; alkaline solutions have numbers above 7 on the pH scale.

anaerobic   Word used to describe an oxygen-free environment or an organism, such as a bacterium, that lives in an oxygen-free environment.

anion   A negatively charged ion.

aquifer   A rock or soil layer that holds useable groundwater.

arable Word used to describe land that is suitable for farming.

atmosphere The gases surrounding a planet or moon.

atom The smallest unit of a chemical element having the properties of that element.

atomic weight The sum of an atom's protons and neutrons (electrons have negligible weight).

bacteria Microscopic, single-celled organisms that are important decomposers.

basalt A dark-colored, relatively dense volcanic rock formed of cooled lava; basalt makes up the bulk of the seafloor.

bauxite Aluminum ore found in tropical soils.

bioaccumulation The accumulation of toxic substances within living organisms.

biodegradable Waste that living organisms can decompose into harmless inorganic materials.

biodiversity The number of different species in a given habitat.

biofuel Living or recently dead organisms or their metabolic products that can be burned to generate power.

biomass The mass of all the living matter in a given area or volume of a habitat.

boreal forest Frigid area of northern Eurasia and Canada dominated by fir trees and diverse mammal life; snow is the dominant precipitation.

carcinogen A substance that causes cancer. A carcinogen affects people who have a genetic predisposition to get the disease more than it does those who do not, except in cases of extreme exposure to the carcinogen.

carrying capacity The maximum number of individuals of a particular species that an environment can support indefinitely.

cathode A positively charged terminal of a battery or voltaic cell.

cation A positively charged ion.

cell The smallest unit of structure and function making up all living things; a life form may be composed of one cell or of many trillions of cells, as in humans and other complex organisms.

chemical bond Mechanism by which atoms come together to form molecules; chemical bonds must be strong enough to keep the atoms together as an aggregate.

chlorofluorocarbon (CFC) A man-made gas that rises into the stratosphere and breaks down ozone.

coal An organic sedimentary rock made of the remains of dead plants that have been compressed; coal is a type of fossil fuel.

creep Slow downhill mass wasting of the shallowest layers of soil, usually found in a humid climate.

DDT Dichlorodiphenyltrichloroethane, a toxic chemical. DDT was a very effective insecticide but was withdrawn from production when its negative effects (and those of its breakdown products) on birds and mammals were realized.

dead zone An ocean region that is hostile to most life; a dead zone is usually caused by eutrophication.

deciduous Word used to describe trees that lose their leaves in the winter to avoid freezing or in the dry season to avoid desiccation; deciduous forests are made mostly of deciduous trees.

decomposer An organism that breaks down the body parts of dead organisms or their waste into nutrients that can be used by other plants and animals.

deforestation The conversion of forest area to nonforest area, often agricultural land or settlements.

desertification The change of semiarid landscapes into desert, sometimes by a change in natural rainfall patterns but often by the misuse of soil or another human activity.

dioxin A toxic chemical (POP) that is a byproduct of the manufacture of other chemicals and has been shown to be hazardous to animals and possibly humans.

disseminated ore An ore deposit in which the valuable mineral is scattered throughout the host rock at very low concentrations.

downwind In the direction toward which the wind is blowing.

dry forest A tropical to subtropical forest that has a long dry season of up to eight months, unlike the tropical rain forest, which has rainfall much of the year.

ecosystem The interrelationships of the plants and animals of a region and the raw materials that they need to live.

ecotourism Tourism that is environmentally and culturally sensitive. Ideally, ecotourism is sustainable; brings a source of income into the region; and educates the tourists on the political, environmental, and social climate of the region and the country.

electron A negatively charged particle that orbits an atom's nucleus.

electrowinning The use of electricity to separate an ore from the solution it is in.

element A substance that cannot be chemically reduced to simpler substances.

endangered species An organism that is threatened with extinction.

endocrine disruptor A compound that interrupts the functions of the endocrine system, often interfering with the sexual development or success of a species; most endocrine disruptors are estrogens or estrogen mimics.

endocrine system The system of the body that controls the internal environment by sending out hormones as chemical messengers.

erosion The movement of sediments from one location to another by water, wind, ice, or gravity.

eutrophication The changes that occur in an aquatic ecosystem when excessive nutrients are released; most commonly, the depletion of oxygen by bacteria.

evapotranspiration The loss of water by evaporation from plants.

evergreen Word used to describe trees and shrubs that have green leaves or needles year round and that shed only when new growth appears; evergreen forests are made primarily of evergreen trees.

extinction A species is extinct if no member survives and reproduces. This can occur in two ways: The species cannot evolve to keep up with a changing environment; it dies out and its genes are lost. Alternatively, the species evolves into another species, and its most useful genes are preserved.

extractive reserve Preserved land in which a few resources are allowed to be taken; Brazil has set up extractive reserves at the request of rubber tappers.

floodplain Level land along a stream formed by the deposition of sediments during flooding.

flow In mass wasting, downhill movement in which the sediment moves as a viscous fluid.

fossil fuels Ancient plants that have decayed and been transformed into a useable fuel, especially coal and petroleum. These fuels are really just stored ancient sunshine.

gemstone A precious or semiprecious stone, often cut and polished for use in jewelry.

gene The unit of inheritance that passes a trait from one generation to the next.

geyser A hot spring in which water periodically spurts upward.

global warming The worldwide rising of average global temperature; the term usually refers to the temperature increases that have taken place in the past 150 years.

greenhouse gases Gases that absorb heat radiated from the Earth. They include carbon dioxide, methane, ozone, nitrous oxide, and chlorofluorocarbons.

Green Revolution Technological changes in agriculture, particularly in grains, that resulted in enormous increases in productivity in the past several decades.

groundwater   Water found in soil or rock beneath the ground surface.

habitat   The environment in which an organism lives, with distinctive features that include such factors as climate, resource availability, predators, and many others.

habitat fragmentation   The breaking apart of a continuous habitat by humans due to the conversion of some of the land to other uses, such as agriculture or urban development.

half-life   The amount of time necessary for half of the nuclei of a radioactive parent isotope to decay to its stable daughter isotope.

heap leaching   A means of removing a valuable metal from its ore rock that involves piling up the crushed rock, then spraying a chemical solution on the pile, allowing it to remove the valuable metal; a cyanide solution is commonly used for this process.

heavy metal   A metal with high weight, especially one that is toxic to organisms.

humus   Partially decomposed organic matter that is found in soil.

hydrocarbon   An organic compound composed of hydrogen and carbon; fossil fuels are hydrocarbons.

hydropower   Power generated from the energy of falling water; hydrologic power.

hydrothermal   Word used to describe hot fluids that can alter rocks and minerals and sometimes create ore deposits.

igneous rock   A rock that forms from a cooling magma: A slow-cooling rock that forms within the Earth's crust is a plutonic igneous rock; a rapidly cooling rock that erupts at the surface and cools is a volcanic igneous rock; igneous rocks are one of the three major rock types.

invasive species   Organisms that are introduced by human activities into a location where they are not native; also called alien species.

ion   An atom that has lost or gained an electron so that it has a positive or negative charge.

irrigation The act of bringing water to cropland that does not get enough water naturally as by canals.

isotopes Two or more atoms of the same element having the same number of protons but a different number of neutrons; thus giving the isotopes different atomic weights.

laterite A mineral- and nutrient-poor soil that is common in the tropics; laterites are not good soils for farming.

litter Partially broken up leaves, flowers, and other organic matter found in soil.

magma Molten rock found below the Earth's surface. At the surface, molten rock is called lava.

mass wasting The erosion of rock and soil down a hillside due to the force of gravity.

metals Chemical elements that are shiny (metallic luster), that lose electrons to form positive ions, and that can conduct heat and electricity.

metamorphic rock Any rock that has been formed by heat, pressure, or deformation (unequally applied pressure); metamorphic rocks are one of the three major rock types.

methane A hydrocarbon gas (CH_4) that is the major component of natural gas. Methane is also a natural component of the atmosphere and a greenhouse gas.

methyl mercury Mercury that bacteria have altered into a toxic organic form.

mineral A naturally occurring, inorganic substance with definite chemical composition and structure; rocks are made of minerals.

molecule The smallest unit of a compound that has all the properties of that compound.

monoculture A method of farming in which only one species of plant is grown.

mudflow Rapid downslope flow of mud and rock.

neutron An uncharged particle found in an atom's nucleus.

nonrenewable resource   A resource that is not replenished on a time-scale that is useful to humans; when it is gone, there is no more; petroleum and many mineral resources are nonrenewable.

nucleus   The center of an atom, composed of protons and neurons.

nutrients   Biologically important elements that are critical to growth or to building shells or bones; important nutrients include nitrogen and phosphorous for plant cell growth; silica and calcium for building shells and skeletons; and nitrates and phosphates for the production of proteins and other biochemicals.

oil shale   Sedimentary rock rich in oil that can be mined using heat and enormous quantities of water.

old-growth forest   A forest that contains trees that have never been logged or that have not been logged for hundreds or thousands of years; old-growth forests are mature ecosystems.

ore   A deposit of valuable mineral or rock that can be profitably mined.

organic farming   Farming that is done without the use of synthetic pesticides or pharmaceuticals.

ozone   A molecule composed of three oxygen atoms and symbolized as O_3. Ozone is a pollutant in the lower atmosphere, but in the upper atmosphere, it protects life on the Earth's surface from the Sun's deadly ultraviolet radiation.

particulates   Solid or liquid pollutants that are small enough to stay suspended in the air. They are generally nontoxic but can seriously reduce visibility.

pathogens   Disease-causing microorganisms including viruses, bacteria, and protozoans.

persistent organic pollutants (POPs)   Chemical substances that persist in the environment, bioaccumulate through the food web, and may damage human health and the environment.

petroleum   A fossil fuel made of hydrocarbons and formed from the transformed bodies of marine organisms.

pH   Numbers from 0 to 14 that express the acidity or alkalinity of a solution. On the pH scale, 7 is neutral, with lower numbers indicating acid and higher numbers indicating base. The most extreme numbers are the most extreme solutions.

photochemical smog   Air pollution that forms when sunlight facilitates the chemical reaction of pollutants such as nitrogen oxides and hydrocarbons.

photosynthesis   The process in which plants use carbon dioxide and water in the presence of sunlight to produce sugar and oxygen. The simplified chemical reaction is $6CO_2 + 12H_2O +$ solar energy $= C_6H_{12}O_6 + 6O_2 + 6H_2O$.

placer   Ore that was deposited by water so that the metals, which are heavier than the other rocky materials, have been concentrated.

pluton   An igneous rock body that is formed from the cooling of a magma inside the Earth's crust.

plutonic rock   A slow-cooling igneous rock that forms within the Earth's crust; e.g., granite.

polyculture   A method of farming in which several species of crops are farmed together.

primary productivity   The creation of organic compounds through the process of photosynthesis.

proton   A positively charged subatomic particle found in an atom's nucleus.

protozoa   Single-celled organisms that do not produce food and that resemble animals.

radioactive decay (radioactivity)   Spontaneous disintegration of the unstable nucleus of an isotope, accompanied by the emission of heat.

renewable resource   A resource that is replaced within a timescale such that it will not be depleted (within reason); tidal energy and salt are renewable resources.

rock slide   Downslope movement of chunks of rock.

runoff   Water that trickles across roadways and rooftops, filters through landfills and soil, and often drains directly into streams or lakes.

salinization   The increase in salt content in soil due to irrigation with brackish water.

sediments   Fragments of rocks and minerals that range in size from dust and clay up to boulders.

sedimentary rock   One of the three major rock types; sedimentary rocks form from compaction and cementation of sediments or from the precipitation of minerals.

selective breeding   The discriminatory breeding of crops for specific purposes.

slash-and-burn agriculture   Form of agriculture in which rain forest plants are slashed down and then burned to clear the land; usually practiced in the tropics.

slide   Mass wasting of a large slab of rock that has broken from the hillside along fractures.

slump   Downslope movement in which a block of soil slips downhill and rotates backwards into the hill.

smelting   The extraction of a metal from ore rock by using heat.

species   A classification of organisms that includes those that can or do interbreed and produce fertile offspring; members of a species share the same gene pool.

subsistence farming   A family farm on which little more is grown than what is needed to feed the farmer's family.

sulfide   A chemical compound in which one or more metal ions is combined with one or more sulfur ions; many valuable ore minerals are in sulfide form.

Superfund   Passed in 1980 and more formally known as the Comprehensive Environmental Response, Compensation, and Liability Act (CERCLA), Superfund provides for the removal of contaminated materials and remedial action for long-term responses for cleanup.

sustainability Word used to describe resource use that does not compromise either the current needs of society for resources or the needs of future generations in search of present economic gain.

tar sands Sands mixed with oil that can be mined using hot water and caustic soda.

temperate forest Cool, wet biome dominated by evergreen (including giant redwood and Douglas fir) forests and deciduous (maple and ash) forests and diverse species of mammals.

topsoil The fertile, upper layer of soil.

tropical rain forest Warm, wet biome of luxuriant forests that shelter much of the world's biodiversity.

urban heat island effect The phenomenon whereby urban areas have higher temperatures than nearby rural areas due to urban areas' absorption of sunlight and release of heat by ground coverings such as concrete and also to their ability to collect waste heat.

urbanization The spread of the urban landscape over the preexisting landscape.

volcanic rock A rapidly cooling igneous rock that forms at or very near the Earth's surface, usually at a volcano.

water cycle The cycling of water between Earth's atmosphere, oceans, and freshwater reservoirs such as glaciers, streams, lakes, and groundwater aquifers.

water table The top of an aquifer; pore spaces above the water table are filled with air and infiltrating water; below the water table, the pore spaces are filled with water.

watershed The area covering a river and all of its tributaries and all of the land that it drains.

weathering Process whereby rocks and minerals at the Earth's surface are broken down or chemically altered by the air, water, or living creatures.

wilderness Land that has not been altered by human activities.

# Further Reading

Davis, Mike. *Planet of Slums*. New York: Verso, 2006.

Grossman, Elizabeth. "Where Computers Go to Die—and Kill." *Salon* (April 10, 2006). Available online. http://www.salon.com/news/feature/2006/04/10/ewaste/index.html. Accessed May 24, 2006.

_____. *High Tech Trash: Digital Devices, Hidden Toxins, and Human Health*. Washington, D.C.: Island Press, 2006.

Johnson, Kirk. "Drier, Tainted Nevada May Be Legacy of Gold Rush." *The New York Times*, December 30, 2005.

Maloney, Peter. "They Tilt and Whirl While Spinning off Cash." *The New York Times,* May 17, 2006.

Manning, Richard. "The Oil We Eat." *Harper's Magazine*, February, 2004. Available online. http://www.harpers.org/TheOilWeEat.html. Accessed May 24, 2006.

McCreery, Laura. "From Mine to Natural Reserve: ROHO Records the Transition." *Bancroftiana. Newsletter of the Friends of the Bancroft Library* 116 (Spring, 2000). Available online. http://bancroft.berkeley.edu/events/bancroftiana/116/fromroho.html. Accessed April 20, 2006.

Moran, Susan. "Panning E-Waste for Gold." *The New York Times*, May 17, 2006.

Perlez, Jane, and Lowell Bergman. "Tangled Strands in Fight Over Peru Gold Mine." *The New York Times*, October 25, 2005.

Perlez, Jane, and Raymond Bonner. "Below a Mountain of Wealth, a River of Waste." *The New York Times*, December 27, 2005.

Perlez, Jane, and Kirk Johnson. "Behind Gold's Glitter: Torn Lands and Pointed Questions." *The New York Times*, October 24, 2005.

Pollan, Michael. *The Omnivore's Dilemma: A Natural History of Four Meals.* New York: Penguin, 2006.

Schneider, Keith. "To Revitalize a City, Try Spreading Some Mulch." *The New York Times*, May 17, 2006.

Steinglass, Matt. "A Swiftly Crumbling Planet." *Salon* (March 14, 2006). Available online. http://www.salon.com/books/review/2006/03/14/davis/index.html. Accessed May 24, 2006.

Wright, Christian L. "Many Little Piggies, Handled with Care." *The New York Times*, May 17, 2006.

Web Sites

Community Supported Agriculture
http://afsic.nal.usda.gov
Information about Community Supported Agriculture, including how to find a farm.

Earth Observing System
http://eospso.gsfc.nasa.gov
From the Goddard Space Flight Center, news stories, in-depth reports, and amazing satellite images that focus on the changes the planet is undergoing.

Michael Pollan
http://michaelpollan.com
A writer specializing in the environmental implications of modern food production and alternatives. Pollan's Web site contains links to many of his articles.

National Sustainable Agriculture Information Service
http://attra.ncat.org
Information about and news on sustainable agriculture, primarily for farmers.

Office of Surface Mining
http://www.osmre.gov/osmreg.htm
A division of the United States Department of the Interior.

Smart Growth America
http://www.smartgrowthamerica.org
Information and news about smart growth in America.

Index

About the Author

DANA DESONIE, PH.D., has written about earth, ocean, space, life, and environmental sciences for more than a decade. Her work has appeared in educational lessons, textbooks, and magazines, and on radio and the Web. Her 1996 book, *Cosmic Collisions*, described the importance of asteroids and comets in Earth history and the possible consequences of a future asteroid collision with the planet. Before becoming a science writer, she received a doctorate in oceanography, spending weeks at a time at sea, mostly in the tropics, and one amazing day at the bottom of the Pacific in the research submersible *Alvin*. She now resides in Phoenix, Arizona, with her neuroscientist husband, Miles Orchinik, and their two children.